WHAT EVERY GOO
SHOULD KNOW

For a complete list of Management Books 2000 titles,
visit our web-site at www.mb2000.com

WHAT EVERY GOOD LAWYER SHOULD KNOW

Iain Campbell B.A.(Hons)

2000

First published in 2000 by Management Books 2000 Ltd
Cowcombe House
Cowcombe Hill
Chalford
Gloucestershire GL6 8HP
Tel. 01285 760 722
Fax. 01285 760 708
E-mail: mb2000@compuserve.com

Printed and bound in Great Britain by Biddles, Guildford

British Library Cataloguing in Publication Data is available
ISBN 1-85252-317-4

WHAT'S IN THIS FOR ME?

START OFF WITH THE RIGHT ATTITUDE AND GET YOURSELF AND YOUR OFFICE READY FOR ACTION!

WHAT ELSE NEEDS LOOKING AT?

AN IN-DEPTH LOOK AT BILLING

YET MORE STUFF TO CHECK OUT!

ADOPT THE CONCEPT THAT IN ORDER TO ACHIEVE UNUSUAL RESULTS, SOMETIMES IT IS NECESSARY TO TAKE UNUSUAL ACTIONS

Note: The text of this book generally avoids the cumbersome 'he or she' construct, but sprinkles the pages liberally with 'he' or 'she' in broadly equal numbers. Of course, either is immediately replaceable with the other. It is hoped that this arrangement will seem sensible.

START OFF WITH THE RIGHT ATTITUDE AND GET YOURSELF AND YOUR OFFICE READY FOR ACTION!

PASSION!!!!

In order to succeed at anything, you must be dedicated. Most lawyers are. However, if you want to have a thriving, buzzing office that will stimulate you and your staff, then you must develop the philosophy that in order to produce unusual results, sometimes you must use unusual methods. You must develop a *passion* for what you do – a real burning desire to help the client in whatever field of law you practice.

You can do this by first of all becoming the very best at what you do. This will give you the confidence to feel passionate about your subject. You also need to be a good communicator. Go on every course you can find to develop your skills in human relations, negotiating, selling, marketing – try the thirteen-week Dale Carnegie human relations course.

Book yourself onto every possible up-dating course for your particular subject that you can find. As with every profession, the people who really succeed are the ones who have all the right information, technical knowledge and communication skills at their fingertips. That must include you.

YOU MUST BE THE VERY BEST AT WHAT YOU DO

With the confidence that you will gain from your learning, you will boost your passion for your work, your clients and your colleagues. This will then filter to the other people you work with – in particular, the non-legal staff.

If the partners come in at 10am and leave at 4pm and bad-mouth their colleagues, the clients, the office and the legal system, then they will have no respect for you or the office they work in. That is no way to act. Such attitudes are more easily noticed and copied than more positive ones – it is up to you to create the right climate for your work. This necessarily entails promoting positive vibes rather than negative or destructive ones.

Get the office to be a fun place to work in. Do things there that aren't the 'usual' activities associated with a lawyer's office. It is not only the public who often have an image of the lawyer's office as being a place full of fusty, gloomy and Dickensian attitudes – many lawyers still see that of themselves. They are too entrenched in their old methods and practices to be a part of the modern world. That must not be you!

Use your imagination – but have a **passion** for it – and fast!

As this book progresses, you will find a large number of immensely practical ideas for improving both your own working life and the services that you offer to your clients. Some of these ideas will strike you as somewhat revolutionary, some as eminently sensible and others as just outside your own personal scale of acceptance. However, they are all applicable somewhere and have been tried and tested with outstanding success. Whichever of the ideas you adopt, adopt them with that passion that marks you out as one of the stars in the legal profession.

No one manages to reach the top of his or her oak tree by sitting on an acorn! Embrace the opportunity to make real changes to your professional life and start to climb your tree branch by branch, idea by idea. That is enough of fanciful metaphors – let's look at some practical ideas to make life easier.

HAVE A GOOD CLEAR OUT

Have a good look round your office. Is it really conducive to 100% efficiency? Are you happy with it? Before you start on a good review of the work methods that you employ, you must get yourself geared up to take on the new approaches detailed in this book.

One of the best and most glorious ways to do so is to clear the decks – really clear the decks. Now, you will need some time to do this so you will have to budget a bit of time for yourself. Let yourself into the office when no one else is around. You won't then be interrupted and you can work faster without the phone ringing. Try a couple of night visits, or if you prefer it, go in on a Sunday. Put some real effort into this exercise, realising that once you have done it, you will be 100% up to date. You will also FEEL so good after you have done it – it will be immensely worthwhile.

Look at your room

Start with your desk. Has it got more on it than a pen, legal pad, time sheet, phone, digital clock and a To-Do list? If so, you've got too much on it. When they come to see you, your clients do not want to see piles of files, correspondence, magazines, law books, screwed-up paper tissues or miscellaneous paperwork. Your clients will not think that you are a busy person if your room looks a mess. They just think that you are inefficient. You may be content with your own particular style of open-cast filing – you may even know where everything is – but your clients will not understand that you like to live in a tip.

- **The desk**
  So start with the desk – clear off stuff that you don't need or want. And have a good look at the top of your desk at last! Remember

that classy green leather top that you haven't seen for a few months? When virtually cleared of accumulated debris, it is ready for the businesslike layout suggested in the section below, 'Laying out your desk to make money' on page 18.

- **The floor and shelves**
  Then look round at the floor and shelves. Have you got piles of Law Society Gazettes there; circulars that were never opened; general clutter that is really of no use to anyone? Well get rid of it all. You're never going to read through those Gazettes, you'll never open the circulars. Chuck them out and give yourself some breathing space.
  Consign all unwanted stuff to black bin-bags – it is extraordinary how much they hold and once thrown in, there is little chance of the items ever being retrieved. You know that it makes sense.

- **Filing cabinets**
  Next comes the filing cabinet(s). Ask yourself – do I really need a filing cabinet in my room? Do I actually need all my files in my room or can they go somewhere else? Perhaps an adjoining room or a secretary's room.
  If you've got to have the cabinets in your room go through them file by file. Check in each one to see if anything still needs to be done and if so, make three piles:

  - the first pile are the files that you can handle on your own

  - the second pile of files are the ones where you need to speak to someone about the matter, so arrange a time to see the appropriate colleague **now** – put it in your diary **now**

  - the third pile is stuff that you've left for days, weeks, months or even years. Maybe it is because you have a mental block about something or there is some reason (no matter what) that is preventing you from finishing the job and moving on.

As soon as the basic sorting is out of the way, your first task must be to tackle these piles of papers. If you leave it more than a day or so, you will never come back to them.

- For the first pile that you can do on your own, get cracking and do whatever needs to be done. This is often helped by making a to-do list, a personal agenda for the next few hours, which can act as a powerful guide to your activities and can really concentrate your thinking and focus.

- The second pile are files where you need to see a colleague to sort out what needs to be done together. Again, a list is helpful here.

- The third pile needs some additional help. Chose someone else from the firm and tell him or her that you are clearing out your filing cabinet and have a problem file where, for example, the estate accounts have never been drafted or the conveyance needs drafting – agree to swap it for one of your colleague's problem files. Or send the file off to someone else to deal with. If it is estate accounts, then get a costs draftsman to do it. If it is drafting documents, try a junior counsel. Whatever you need to do – do it, but do it **now!**

The filing cabinet should now hold items that you are currently working on and you should **know** for each file **precisely** where you are on each matter. You will get a feeling of tremendous relief once you have done this.

- **Decor and layout**
  After the paperwork is sorted into sensible piles, have another look round the room to see if you can improve the rest of the place at all.

  - Does it need repainting?

- Have you got some pictures you could hang up or should you replace the rather tired ones that are there already?

- Could you make the room look more appealing?

- Have you got rows of law books covering the walls of the room? If so move them out. By all means keep a few books that you use regularly on some shelves but keep them stored unobtrusively. Your office needs to look welcoming. Clients are put off by loads of leather-bound law books. So get rid of them (the books, that is – not the clients!).

Whatever you do to your room, remember that you have to feel professional and confident in it and your clients must feel comfortable and well catered for also. It is a statement about **you**.

THE FIRST IMPRESSION AND THE RECEPTION

Have a think about this for a minute. Imagine that you're a **client** and you're visiting a lawyer for the first time.

It is 2pm on a hot Summer's afternoon. You've got an appointment to see a solicitor at a firm you have never been to before. You are worried. You don't know what to expect. You haven't met the lawyer before. You don't know if he will relate to you or be competent or think you're a complete jerk. You think you have a major problem and desperately seek some advice or preferably a solution. You rehearse what you are going to say to him for the fiftieth time. You wonder if it sounds plausible. You are determined to get it over in a logical way but you're so nervous you don't know if you will be able to and that thought is making you feel worse.

It's a hell of a drive to this firm. You eventually arrive at the firm's car park. There's only one space left. It's next to a skip where builders are chucking out old bricks. You know that when you return to your car there will be a fine film of brick dust all over it.

This parking space is the farthest one from the firm's front door. You walk to the reception area, checking your watch for the umpteenth time and you breathe a sigh of relief that at least you're not late. In fact you're ten minutes early. Perhaps the journey wasn't that bad after all.

You open the reception door. The place smells smoky. There's one receptionist - she's on the phone. She points to the phone to show you that she is speaking to someone and then holds up her hand to stop you saying anything. Whilst carrying on the conversation she mouths, "I'll be with you in a minute." Finally, the phone call finishes.

"Hello," she says as the phone rings again. Her hand goes up again. You stand there waiting.

The call finishes and you quickly say, "I'm John Whiteley - I'm here to see Mr Dickinson."

"Have you got an appointment?"

"Yes ... Mr Dickinson wrote to me to ask me to come at 3pm."

She looks in some book or other. "Are you sure you've got an appointment?"

"Yes."

"Oh well, you're not in my book," she says. "That's always happening. The secretaries are supposed to tell me who's coming so I'll know, but they mostly never bother. Well, sit over there and I'll see if I can find Mr Dickinson."

You sit down in an area out of sight of the Receptionist. There is a coffee table there with ragged copies of Punch, none of which is less than two years old. Fifteen minutes go by. You don't know if she has found Mr Dickinson or confirmed that the appointment is correct. Anxiously you go back to the receptionist.

"Oh yes, sorry!" she says. "I tracked him down to the toilets. He says that Maureen his secretary has left your name off the diary list for today. But he'll see you in a minute after he's made some important calls."

You wonder if you're important.

Another twenty minutes go by. You go back to the reception desk.

"Oh sorry! Mr Dickinson has buzzed for you but I can't find anyone to take you to his room."

"I'll go on my own," you suggest.

"Oh no, sorry. Security says no-one is to go upstairs without being accompanied by a firm member. Confidentiality or something. Hang on I'll see what I can do."

She broadcasts on an intercom system – "Doreen here, can anyone take a client to Mr Dickinson's room?"

A secretary walks in the main door and hears the announcement.

"I'll take him up. I'm going for coffee anyway," she says.

You walk behind this girl. She says nothing. You arrive at a door. She points to it and says, "That's Mr Dickinson's office."

You knock, but hear no response. Gingerly you open the door. Mr Dickinson is on the phone. He's seated at his desk and has his jacket off. He doesn't stand but continues with his phone call.

You look at his desk. It is piled high with files, Law Society Gazettes and miscellaneous paperwork. The colour of the desk-top is not apparent because of the mass of material piled upon it. Mr Dickinson finishes his call. He points to a hard-back seat, thrusts his arm over the papers and says, "Mr Whiteson – sorry about the mess-up – just can't get the staff these days. Now, what can I do for you?"

"It's Whiteley," you reply.

Now contrast that with this:

It's back to 2.45 pm on that hot sunny day. You arrive at the firm's car park and you're looking for somewhere to park. There's a space with a sign marked 'Reserved for Mr Whiteley'.

It's right next door to the main reception entrance. You get out of the car and walk into reception. The glass door has a coloured notice which says 'Welcome to Bornter and Partners'. Above the receptionist's head is an electronic display board that cannot be missed. It shows, 'Welcome to our Guests of the Day – Mr Whiteley, Mr Bannister and Mrs Burton'.*

You walk up to the Reception desk. There are two receptionists. One of them is on the phone but the other says, "Hello. Mr Whiteley is it?" You nod.

"Mr Dickinson is expecting you, please take a seat and I'll tell him that you're here. Meanwhile would you like to help yourself to an ice-cold drink."

The seating area is well lit, has three current newspapers, a clutch of current monthly magazines, a bowl of wrapped boiled sweets and an assortment of cold drinks nestling in a tray of ice-cubes with sparkling glasses.

Along one wall is a bank of television screens with earphones, showing some of the work which the partnership has done for clients.

At 3pm precisely, one of the receptionists asks you to accompany her to Mr Dickinson's room. You do so. She keeps eye contact with you and talks to you as you go.

The receptionist opens Mr Dickinson's door. He has already moved to the front of his desk and greets you with a firm handshake. His desk is uncluttered. He has on it a digital clock, a modern reading light, a phone, a legal pad and pen and a Time Sheet. His computer is on a side desk with his dictation equipment. Not a file can be seen.

* Of course, a degree of discretion must be exercised when displaying people's names for all and sundry to see (especially if members of the public can see the display from the street). Quite a few clients will not want the world and his wife to know that they are visiting a solicitor.

From these two scenarios, we can see the importance of the **first impression** on the new client. No legal advice has so far been dispensed but the client has built up an experience of the firm by the way he was treated. All that has happened in the second scenario that is different from the first, is that the potential client – and remember he isn't a client yet – has been treated with some respect. The firm acts as if he's an important person and, make no mistake, the client **is** an important person. He's the **sole** reason that you're there. It's your job to super-please him.

> ## YOU DON'T GET A SECOND CHANCE TO MAKE A FIRST IMPRESSION

That old saying is so true. The potential client will be looking forward – maybe with some trepidation and/or optimism – to his first meeting with the firm and his experiences will be remembered.

So the message here is that the impression your client has about the firm commences even before he sees the lawyer. Think about the potential new client's first visit to your firm and how you would like him to be treated.

This thought can be moved back a further step in time, because the impressions start to build **before** your client even calls. He or she will have made a choice of your firm as opposed to other local firms and this will be biased or influenced by impressions already gained from conversations, advertisements, literature, newspaper reports and a myriad other sources. If those combine to create a favourable impression, then you have a new client – if not, not. More about these points later ...

LAYING OUT YOUR DESK TO MAKE MONEY

You will spend hundreds of hours at your desk, so organise and arrange the furniture to be efficient for you. The layout of the room needs to assist you in offering the best possible service to your clients and that means that you and they must be comfortable, both in terms of the furniture available and in respect of the professional atmosphere and overall, physical pleasantness of the room.

As you sit at your desk, immediately in front of you should be a legal note pad. If you are right handed, to the right of you will be your time sheet and digital clock. To the left of your legal pad should be your telephone and the 'things-to-do' pad.

- The legal pad is for note-taking.

- The time-sheet will detail the time spent on the activities of the day.

- The digital clock will help you time all those activities and saves constantly looking at your wrist watch.

- The things-to-do pad should contain all those matters which you need to attend to that day. However, this should not be within reading distance of your client or it might appear that she is merely being squeezed in between other clients.

On a smaller desk to one side should be your computer and a picture of your wife/husband/partner and children if you have any. An in-tray of correspondence or other items that are to be attended to can be sited alongside the computer but out of sight of the client.

With this set-up, you are ready to make maximum use of your time and make the most money.

A family photo?

The reason that the photo is there is not only to remind you of some of the joys in life but it is an essential requirement when coming to billing. There is a huge tendency amongst lawyers to bill too low on the basis that the bill 'sounds' too high. If you have a picture of of your loved ones to look at as you bill, and they are dependent on the income you produce, you will find that your tendency to under-bill becomes dramatically less!

THOSE SILLY REASONS

Not much has been written in this country about why we choose a particular lawyer – why one is chosen and not another. Mostly the choice is made because the person was recommended to you in the first place. Lawyers like to think it is because of their expertise or the fact that they can do a better job than another lawyer down the road. But often the choice is because of silly reasons that never appear in a survey.

Think about it. Why do you like your favourite restaurant? Why doesn't everybody like it? Why do your prefer one dry cleaner to another?

Often, neither of these businesses is chosen because of their cheapness. Often it is to do with the personal attributes of the owner.

> I have been twice to a Chinese Restaurant that is 35 miles from my home. My brother invited me the first time and the food was excellent, but what I most remember is the husband and wife team who ran the place. They believed in customer satisfaction. Not as a gimmick but because they genuinely liked people and really enjoyed providing a good night for them. As a result, the business premises have doubled in size in a matter of a few years.
>
> My brother didn't manage to return to the place for a year because of a new-born child. I went with him on his next visit and he was treated like a long-lost friend. The owners wanted to know about the baby and as a result of this attention, many members of my family and my brother's fellow work-people have visited the place.

These personal feelings of appreciation will filter through into the business world. These small reasons why you visit a particular place or return to a particular service provider will be the same as those for a business. Provide a first-class service to one client and the word will spread - louse it up and that will spread too. You have a choice.

EXPECTATIONS AND PERCEPTIONS – THE VITAL DIFFERENCE!!

Clients will compare what their *expectations* were against what they *perceive* they have received. It is essential to know the difference between what the client expects from your service with what they *perceive* that they actually had from you. You may notice that I do not say with what they actually received. It is not what they actually got that is important here. It is what they perceived they received.

You need to ensure that it is their perceptions that you are managing. So what you must do is super-please your clients. You must make them so delighted with the service that you provide that they will be happy to recommend you to anyone.

Here are a few ways to do that:

- Return all calls promptly.

- Send your clients copies of everything that comes into the office affecting them – especially documents of any kind. They will then realise quite clearly that you are working hard for them if they can recognise that you have a wealth of documents on file.

- Make sure at the start that you have agreed in writing how you will bill them and then do so in the way that you have agreed.

- Do not give your clients any unpleasant surprises.

- Go and see the client at his or her place of work. You will be surprised at how much this is appreciated. Also you will be amazed at the sort of additional work you can ferret out from both the client and others in the workplace. For business clients this is an absolute **must!**

- Make house calls. See clients at home, especially if they have any difficulty in getting into the office to meet you there.

- If your client has an appointment to see a medical specialist that you have arranged or some other expert or adviser, then go along with them. You do not always need to stay for the full session. Tell the client that you will receive a report from the expert. You can then simply introduce the expert to the client and go. It will give your clients a feeling that you are in there together and they are not just fighting battles on their own.

- If you are acting for a client who has had an accident, always, always, always visit the scene with the client.

THE MAGIC OF RAPPORT

This is a secret that should be known by all lawyers - but isn't. In order to get the confidence of a new client – or indeed anybody – you need to establish rapport with that person. Often you need to do it fairly quickly because time is limited and the client's time is important. Also time is money.

There are two ways to establish rapport. People buy <u>people</u> first and whatever else after. So you need to persuade the client to buy **you** before they'll be the least bit interested in what you have to say.

Establishing rapport – 1

The first way is to agree with whatever the client says. Take a minute to think about this.

Imagine that you are seated next to somebody at a dinner party and you put forward a suggestion about the way that the local school is being run and that person then says, "Well, that's the dumbest thing I've heard in a long time. At the school down the road, we tried that two years ago and failed. I'm surprised that you're not more up to date with your thinking." You probably won't like that person because he doesn't agree with what you strongly believe in.

Now suppose that you are at another dinner party and you offer a work suggestion to the person sitting next to you and he says, "That sounds brilliant! We've been trying to find a solution to that for two years and I think you've set us off in the right direction." This time, you think that this person likes you and your ideas – he's obviously well educated and astute.

> **PEOPLE LIKE PEOPLE
> WHO ARE LIKE THEY ARE**

What that second person said was that your idea is a good one. He is thinking in the same way you are. There is a bond, a rapport there that you can build on. He is a little bit like you so it must be easy to get to know him and once you have got to know him, then the relationship is easier. You're not talking to a stranger but a colleague or a friend.

As far as the new client is concerned, rapport can be used to agree with the client. However, that is not always possible because you know the law and you are in the position to tell the client that he or she is wrong about a particular matter. But – nobody likes to be told that they are wrong, so what do you do?

Establishing rapport – 2

Here is a second way of establishing early rapport. Instead of saying, "No you are wrong," you say, "I can understand how you came to that conclusion", or "I can understand why you feel like that", or "I can understand why you did that."

Empathise with your clients, **understand** why they did a certain thing and move on from there. Empathy has been defined as a willingness to stand in someone else's shoes (or see things from their point of view) but without wishing to stay there permanently.

You should never tell clients that they were stupid to even think about the course of action they undertook.

So, *agree* with your clients or, if you cannot agree, you can at least *understand* why the particular course of action was taken. In that way, you will develop rapport and your clients will be able to take whatever else you tell them because they will feel that they have a friend, an ally who understands them.

THE POWER OF 'WE'

When you are talking to a client, use the word 'we' a lot. If you keep saying things such as 'you've got a problem', the client may become discouraged and not see you as being on the same side. Instead use 'we'. You need to show that you are both together dealing with the matter – that he is not on his own. Also avoid using the word 'problem' – it has a negative connotation that is very disheartening for the client. Use the word 'solution' a lot. Talk about how 'we' can help with finding solutions.

Use 'we' a lot as in – 'we'll go and visit the scene of your accident together', and 'don't worry – we'll see the doctor together for the first few minutes.'

There is a great deal of mileage in the old adage 'a trouble shared is a trouble halved' and many clients will feel considerable relief when they share the problem with you. Even if the matter is not contentious, the mere fact of having spoken about it with a professional advisor will often reduce their tensions and will create a sound basis for working together. The word 'we' has strong overtones of salvation and joint responsibility for success.

DIFFERENTIATION – SERVICE

One factor that will make any enterprise succeed where others flounder is differentiation – making their service different from the others to such a degree that potential clients or customers come flocking to the door. Being different, or being better, are the aims and clients will seek out the firm that offers the best deal, the best service, the best results.

As an example, let us consider some clothing retailers and the way they differentiate themselves from one another.

- Marks & Spencer sell clothes that are top quality, well-made and with a money-back guarantee. If you don't like your purchases, you can return them for whatever reason.

- The chain of Next shops sells more expensive clothes that cater for the person who is willing to spend a bit more on being fashionable. Their windows look entirely different from Marks & Spencer's.

- At the top end of the market are the exclusive designer-label clothes that sell for hundreds if not thousands.

All these companies have a particular image and want to differentiate themselves from their competitors so that there is no possibility that you would mistake one type of retail outlet from another. This is something that lawyers should also be looking to do.

Let's face it, one conveyance is very much like another, one will is very much like another and certainly has no difference in the minds of the client. Consequently, what lawyers must do is differentiate themselves on the basis of the service *process* not the service *outcome*. In other words, the whole interaction with your client on each matter is something which should be looked at and carefully managed, from the initial contact through the lifetime relationship that you have with that client.

It is quite possible to sell a terrible product extremely well – it is also possible to sell a brilliant product in an appalling way. Imagine a doctor with superb bedside manner and complete charm diagnosing a patient's illness entirely wrongly. Likewise imagine a vendor selling Rolex watches by saying, "'ere, guv, wanna fancy ticker?" You need to take the best of both situations. It is the difference between the 'process' of delivering legal advice and the 'content' – the advice itself. Of course, your clients will want you to offer good advice (that is what they are paying for) but they will more immediately be affected by the way in which you do it. If your 'process' is good, then the 'content' is more likely to be accepted – but it had still better be good!

DIFFERENTIATION — PRODUCT

Lawyers do not sell products. What they have for sale is intangible. It cannot be touched, weighed or smelled (even if nasty Norman says that your service stinks!). The intangibility of services offered is a challenge to the law firm. However, firms do produce some tangible material in the form of literature. You must therefore try to find ways of differentiating the firm with those few paper products that you do produce.

Using your literature is an ideal way to make your firm stand out from the crowd. Your letter heading should be the first item to which you should pay attention and from there, you can have an appealing design for all your paperwork – bills, brochures, information packs, leaflets and so on. Hire a graphic designer to come up with some new designs for you. Use the imagination of the designer and see how far you can go. Forget what the competition will think about it. You are in business after all, and you need to be attractive to clients – you do not want them to seek advice from the other lawyers down the road.

FORGET FILE-DRIVEN – BECOME CLIENT-DRIVEN

Most lawyers are conscientious and spend a great deal of time on their files. After all, it is their bread and butter. However, as a result, every matter they deal with is seen *in relation to a particular file*. No attempt is made to look at the broader picture. This is a habit that lawyers will have to cease if they are to continue and thrive.

A file is a problem requiring a solution or more than one solution. However, the client has many requirements and must be serviced as a life-long client, not just as a will client or a matrimonial client and filed away and forgotten once that particular job has been done. We need to look at the whole process of client satisfaction and manage the service element of our work, not just the outcome. Clients are used to expecting a high level of service from other service providers – for example banks and building societies – and they must receive a high level of service from their lawyers. If we choose not to provide such service, then we will lose our clients to somebody else who *cares.*

An example can be drawn here from the medical services. All too often, maybe under the pressure of increasing case-loads, patients are referred to as 'the haemorrhage' or 'the bowel job' without any consideration of the fact that they are people with feelings and fears. It is not right that people should be categorised as if they were mere numbers or ciphers. It may be more convenient to refer to 'the bowel job' than to remember that it is Mrs Bloggs that is lying there on the operating table, but it is rather demeaning and mechanistic.

Similarly, you must avoid saying that you "had another matrimonial in today", when you mean that you saw Mrs Wilderspoon who happened to be concerned about a matrimonial matter.

So how do you do it?

The client needs to know what other work you do. So many clients go to more than one firm because they do not know that their present firm offers a complete range of work – 'I thought you only did conveyancing'.

• Spend a little time in producing an appealing and informative brochure that outlines the range of services that you provide and post one out to *every* client so that they will know what sort of work your firm does. This does not need to be over-elaborate or super-snazzy, but it should reflect the diversity of your services and the fact that you can offer a better, more professional and more caring service than others in the area.

- The whole service process must be something that the entire office is involved in. Every member of the firm, from the senior partner to the most recently appointed junior in the post-room must know how to please the client and be there to help service the client.

- Seek all the important information from the client right at the start – find out the full name and date of birth; establish details of the wife/husband/partner and children; whether they are employed or self-employed; and as many financial details you can. Regularise it by completing a Client Personal Record Form. Then create a sound databank on your computer. With the right information to hand, you will then be in a much better position to cross-sell when the time comes.

With the brilliance of electronic notebooks such as the Psion, it is easy to compile a sound and comprehensive database about your personal client group. Data can be transferred from computer to notebook very simply. The ease with which you can access data is exceptional and you can carry this small 'filing cabinet' of relevant facts and figures with you – giving you instant information no matter where you may be.

THE INTERVIEW

By the time the client reaches your room, he or she may well be nervous, having practised what to say to you for days in advance and once again in the waiting room.

The client is nervous, concerned and wants to be liked. Remember – people like people who are like they are. So establish some rapport with the client. Here are a few golden rules for the interview:

- **Be prompt.**
  If you've arranged to see your client at 10am then see him at that time. Not before and certainly *not* after. Some lawyers seem to think that clients have nothing to do other than sit in their waiting rooms. Clients *do not like it!* It is discourteous to keep clients there beyond the appointed time. If it really is unavoidable (and you'd better have a good reason to keep fee-paying clients waiting) then get someone to tell your clients what is happening. Keep them informed. Never let them feel that they have been forgotten. They will understand as long as they know what's going on.

- **Welcome your clients**
  Preferably meet your clients in the waiting area and escort them to your office. If you cannot do that or it is impractical, then come out from your desk and give your client a firm handshake and show him where to sit. Thank him for coming.
  A very useful introductory technique is to spend a short time (one minute maximum) in inconsequential conversation about the weather or some such. This allows you and the other person to recognise the other's voice and appearance before the real nitty-gritty of the interview starts. Once this chatty start is over, the two of you can launch very successfully into a serious dialogue.

- **First Impression**
  The first thing you say to your new client is vital. It will be his first impression of you and he will remember it for a long time. If you already know in broad terms what is the reason for the visit, then be sure to say, as soon as he sits down, that *no matter what* the particular problem is that is worrying him, the two of you will sort it out together. *This is a very powerful statement.* It shows that you care. The problem has been relieved slightly already because

29

he has heard you say that you are there to help him sort it out. He has a lawyer helping him and the *two* of you will be working on it. He is bound to feel much better and you do not even know what the depth of the problem is yet. This approach creates a fantastic start to your relationship with the new client.

- **Clear the desk**
  There is nothing more of a pain to a client than a lawyer who leaves heaps of rubbish and files concerning other people's cases all over his desk. It does not give a good impression to the client. Maybe you can survive easily amidst your open-cast filing, but such a lack of organisation could well indicate to your client that you have a similar mind – cluttered, disorganised and unreliable. So clear the desk. Have just your notepad and timesheet ready.

- **Control the interview**
  Use mirroring techniques to gain rapport with your clients. Listen to what they are saying and try to use some of the phrases or words that they use. They will see you as a little bit like themselves if you use words which they use. Take the notes that you need and tell the client what you are doing – do not make note-taking a furtive or behind-the-hand exercise.

- **L i s t e n !**
  It is not merely enough to hear what is being said to you in an interview, you must listen with your 'third ear' to actually register and comprehend what is being said. You need to be able to listen **creatively** and **consciously** in order to take in the words and the **meanings** of what is being presented to you. You owe it to your client to have everything open – eyes, ears and mind.

- **Discuss fees and give clients the information required by the Law Society Code**
  At the end of the interview you should be in a position to sort out a fee. If you cannot agree a fixed fee or for some reason a fixed fee is not appropriate, then the basis of calculation should be

explained. The Law Society has Rules about this so check out the *Solicitors' Practice Cost Information and Client Care Amendment Rules 1999* and the *Solicitors' Cost Information and Client Care Code 1999*. At this point, information about (a) the cost of the work (b) who will be responsible for the client's work and (c) details of the firm's complaints procedure need to be given to the client.

- **Anything else?**
  Ask your clients if they want to talk about anything else. You may have picked up in the interview that they need advice about an unrelated topic that they had never thought about. Make the suggestion to your client and recommend that some thought should be given to it. Make contact with your client later on to follow this idea up.

- **What next?**
  Always conclude an interview by making it quite clear to your clients what you will be doing on their behalf. Write to confirm what happened at the interview, along lines similar to this (but note that the sections are only numbered so that we can study the content of the letter!):

ABC SOLICITORS

Dear Mr Potter   Today's date

Thank you for taking the time to come and see me today.[1] I was pleased to meet you for the first time.[2]

You have said[3] that you are proposing to take on a lease of some new business premises to expand your manufacturing base. You indicated that the length of the lease is 14 years with an initial rent of £230,000 per annum.

You have asked me[4] to handle the conveyancing work for you. I am pleased to confirm[5] that I will be delighted to act on your behalf. I have already contacted the estate agents by telephone to tell them that I am acting for you and I have written a letter which I have also faxed to the Lessors' Solicitors requesting the initial paperwork.

As soon as I hear from them, I will let you have an initial Report[6] with a further more substantive Report as soon as all my searches and enquires are completed. As we discussed today[7], the Business Tenancy Legislation is very strict on time limits. Once you take on the Lease, it will be important to ensure that you stick rigidly to the provisions in the Lease and the Statutory Provisions which cover them.

Once you have completed your new Lease, I will remind you of the various Rules so that you can make the necessary diary notes.

I confirm that my firm's fees[8] for your new Leasehold investment will be £6500 plus VAT and the various disbursements we talked about which are .... You have agreed to pay £3000 within the next 7 days and the remainder on completion of the new Lease.

I enclose two copies of my firm's Representation Agreement covering the matters we have discussed. Could I ask you to read it through and let me know if you have any queries. Assuming you are happy, then please sign the Agreement on page 4 and return one copy to me.

As I told you, I am the Partner who heads the Commercial Section here[9]. Please feel free to contact me at any stage. My home phone number is 01234 5678910 and I will be happy to take your call. (If you call me at home you may like to know that my wife's name is Sheila) My e-mail address is JT@ xyzmail.com

If you have any difficulty contacting me, then please contact my colleague John Watts. His home phone number is 01234 5678911 and his partner's name is Amy. His e-mail address is JW@zyx-mail.com. He is a Solicitor and will be familiar with your Leasehold acquisition. My secretary Jane Horlocks you will also find very helpful. Her personal extension number at the office is 234.

If anything in the Representation Agreement or any of the above is not clear[10], then please feel free to contact me at any time. You may like to know that we operate a Client Complaints' Procedure here. Naturally I hope that you will have no cause to complain – however should you have a problem that you feel hasn't been addressed by me or my team, then please feel free to contact our Managing Partner, Thomas Quillan, who I am sure you will find most helpful and sympathetic. His private extension is 4356.

I also enclose an Information Pack[11] giving further details of the other services the firm has to offer. The Pack also gives details of the way the firm is run and I am sure you will find the information quite helpful. Again if you have any particular questions, then any of my team will be happy to speak to you.

Yours sincerely,

Let us take an analytical look at the numbered points in the letter:

(1) *'Thank you'* – remember to say thank you. Mr Potter was not obliged to see you – he could just as easily have gone somewhere else. Also – *'see me today'* – make sure you write the letter the day you meet him, so that he will receive it the next working day. It is important that you impress on the client straightaway that you can do things quickly.

(2) *'for the first time'* – this confirms that the interview was your first meeting.

(3) *'You have said'* – you are repeating the facts that *he* has given you. It is important that you have them correct. If he thinks that you have reported them wrongly, then he has a chance to come back to you to correct anything. It will cut down any thoughts of a negligence claim on the basis that you got the facts wrong.

(4) *'You have asked me to handle the conveyancing work'* – this clearly confirms that the client has *instructed* you, and that there is no possibility of his saying (a) that you hadn't been asked to commence work and (b) that all that he wanted was a quote.

(5) *'I am pleased to confirm that I will be delighted to act'* – tells him that you welcome him as a new client. *'I have already ...'* – tells him that you have already done as much as you can do. Try to do something while your client is still in the room with you. Clients like lawyers who actually **do** something immediately, no matter how small.

(6) *'I will let you have an initial Report'* – tells the client what to expect. Commercial clients love reports, so tell Mr Potter that he will be getting one soon and another one later.

(7) *'As we discussed'* – reminds the client what you both said. This will remove any possibilities of his coming back and saying that you never told him. Here you have captured it in writing. *'Once you take on the Lease'* – tells the client that you will be looking out for his interest even after the Lease has been completed. Show him that you care about his position. Super-please him.

(8) *'I confirm that my firm's fees ...'* – confirms what you have agreed about fees. Tell him that VAT and disbursements are on top of your fees to comply with the Law Society's Guidelines and send him your Representation Agreement (otherwise known as your Non-Contentious Business Agreement) in duplicate. Ask to have one sent back from him signed, and make sure he has a copy of it.

(9) *'I am the Partner who heads the Commercial Section'* – reminds Mr Potter what status you have and who else will be dealing with the matter. This complies with the Law Society's Guidelines. *'My home number is ...'* – gives him your home phone number and the name of your partner. He will be a lot more comfortable with this information and he will be **really** grateful that you have given it to him. However, he will probably not use it but you have shown that you regard him and his work as being important. You've super-pleased him. Give him as much information about contacting the office as you can, including e-mail addresses, especially for Commercial Clients.

(10) *'If anything in the Representation Agreement ... is not clear'* – gives the client a chance to say that he doesn't understand something. You want a client who comprehends precisely what advice you give him. This will also back up your indemnity policy if the client says that you didn't make things clear. *'Client Complaints Procedure'* – complies with the Law Society Client Care Code which requires that you give details of the firm's complaints procedure to the client.

(11) *'I also enclose an Information Pack'* – Send Mr Potter the Firm's information pack, suitably tailored to the needs of **this particular commercial client**. He should be aware of the other services offered by the firm, so include in the pack details of specific services that might be appropriate for his type of business or perceived legal needs. Ask him if he has any questions about the contents of the pack. This is where you can start cross-selling for the first time with this client.

This form of letter is helpful to the client but also gives you a form of protection for the future. The idea is to have satisfied clients who are super-pleased with the service you give. Sending them written advice and information is one of the best ways of ensuring that you do this and it cuts down any misunderstandings and claims on your indemnity policy.

You should also check out the *Solicitors' Practice (Costs Information and Client Care) Amendment Rules 1999* and the *Solicitors' Cost Information and Client Care Code 1999*. Details of what you must tell or inform the client are detailed there.

Also there are specimen letters covering both contentious and non-contentious matters which you can use. The wording is somewhat legalistic but the information should be used in your Representation Agreement. (See the *Law Society Gazette* 21st April 1999 for a pull-out containing the full Rules and Code.)

TREAT THE CLIENT AS A LIFETIME CLIENT

Forget the idea that your client is here just for one transaction. You must see every client as a client for life. If he or she comes to you for advice on an employment matter at the age of 25 years, then over that person's lifetime, advice could be needed on moving house several times, wills, financial services, disputes with neighbours ... the list goes on. From this, you can clearly see that the one-off transaction client should not be the norm. You should build a bank of clients who will be loyal to you.

Realise that the client who is a lifetime client is worth much more to the firm than the one-off transaction. It costs **much** less to market your services to your existing clients than it does to find new ones. So you must treat each new client as a potential lifetime client.

Suppose that you have a 23 year-old client. Throughout her lifetime she will be moving seven times on average and will require assorted legal advice during her life.

If you make a rough calculation as to the lifetime worth of this client to the firm, the figures could look like the simple sum opposite.

So this client's lifetime worth to the firm is £15,000. If you look at it that way you can see the benefit of keeping clients and regarding them not simply as clients for one-off transactions, but for life.

Conveyancing fees	3000
Consumer advice	1200
Wills	300
Financial services	7000
Disputes	2000
Miscellaneous advice	1500
Total	**£15,000**

But it doesn't stop there. You can take the analysis to another level. It is hoped that super-pleased clients will recommend your services to others, maybe as many as ten other new clients. Those ten others could provide a further £15,000 x 10 (£150,000) worth of business. That, added to the existing client's lifetime worth, means that your income over the years is now £165,000 from those clients.

You can also go to yet a further level. Those ten new clients could introduce a further ten clients each, thereby increasing the income by a further £1,500,000. This is then added to the existing £165,000 and you have the grand total of £1,665,000! Now if you think about your clients in these terms, it puts an entirely different slant on the situation. It makes your clients become even more important. It makes the reasons for super-pleasing your clients **paramount**!

THE 'IT'LL DO' ATTITUDE

Picture the scene – there is a tiny mistake in a letter to a client. Her name is spelled incorrectly. It is 5pm and your secretary is dying to get home. Do you send the letter out as it is because, after all, you can read it and **'it'll do'**, or do you insist on having it redone?

Have it re-done every time! There is no contest.

You must **not** send clients letters which contain mistakes. It shows that the firm has a couldn't-care-less attitude which will reflect, so far as your client is concerned, on the quality of its legal work as well.

Also it is most discourteous to the client – especially if the client's name is wrong. If it is wrong, it **must** be done again.

One of the banes of modern-day communications is the ubiquitous spell-checker found on all word processing systems. Do bear in mind that these systems are stupid! Okay, they can check spellings but, if a word exists but is the wrong word in the context of your letter, it will pass it as correct.

Often the consequences can be dire – even more so in the legal world where the words have to be correct. Therefore, there is a strong onus on writers of letters and other documents in your firm to not only write originally in good English, but also to check most carefully when the piece comes back from the word processing pool.

> There was the case of the senior executive who contacted a correspondent in high dudgeon to complain of being patronised. He had received a letter that concluded, "We look forward to hearing from you son." Spell-checker said it was good enough! Such a pity that the originator of the letter did not read it carefully before posting it.

The 'it'll do' syndrome sadly exists in fields other than letter-writing. Often an internal memo or a hurried phone call to a colleague can be dashed through with scant regard for precision, when mistakes can occur. An untidily assembled batch of papers can look very careless when twenty seconds of attention would make so much difference. 'It'll do' will not do.

Beware also the wretched habit of according less attention to people lower down in the hierarchy than you are. Often their grasp of technical or legal detail is not as keen as yours and there is a tendency amongst professionals to show an unwarranted superiority on occasions under the banner of 'they're not worth the fuss', or 'it'll do'. Again, it won't do.

RETURN THE CLIENT'S PHONE CALLS

It is a constant source of amazement how often clients' phone calls are not returned within the hour or not returned that day, or in some case **never** returned. *If you learn only one thing from this book, it must be to return clients phone calls promptly.* Promptly means within half an hour or, better still, within 15 minutes. Your client is sitting at home waiting for you to return his call. He is not making any other calls because he doesn't want the line to be busy when you do call. He's worried, anxious and concerned. His belief is that a quick call to his lawyer will sort out the immediate problem. If he doesn't manage to have that call, he will not be a happy client.

However, it must be accepted that you are not always in the office – you may be at court or in a meeting or out of the office – but someone **must** phone the client back and deal with the query that is causing such immediate concern.

The call return is **vital** to the client. Lawyers don't realise how important this aspect of the job really is. So organise the office to ensure that **someone** is returning those calls.

How about advertising the fact that you will return calls within ten minutes and putting a guarantee on it that if you fail to do this, the client will be entitled to an hour's free advice!
SUPER-PLEASE THE CLIENT

Nowadays, it is not enough to please your clients – you really do have to **super-please** them. All your clients must be really pleased with the service that they receive from you.

Here are a few ways to super-please your clients:

- Return all phone calls promptly.
- Add value to the service you provide by showering the client with information-packed papers.
- Keep all promises.
- Ask questions to find out all your client's needs, not just the legal ones.

- Develop a case plan or strategy for each client and give the client a copy of it.
- Define clearly your responsibilities.
- Define the client's responsibilities.
- Do not just meet your client's expectations – exceed them.
- Understand and define your client's objectives and include them in the case plan.
- Prepare a Representation Agreement for each client and get the client to sign it.
- Telephone your clients when they least expect it.

QUALITY

Quality is vital, vital, vital.

- Your **service** must be **high** quality.
- Your **products** must be **excellent** quality
- Your **advice** must be **exceptional** quality
- Your **people** must be **superb** quality.

But nowadays, a quality product is just a **starting point**. You cannot differentiate your service by saying that it is a quality service.

Clients **already expect** a quality service. They think that is what they are going to get anyway. Just because you have registered for ISO 9001 doesn't mean that you can sit back. That is just the start of a long road of improving everything you do. You will find that clients – and especially your corporate clients – will expect you to have ISO 9001. In fact some corporate clients will choose not to do business with you unless you do have it.

TELL THE CLIENT

Whatever we are involved in at the office or in our own social lives, if we know what's going on, then we are much more content and happy with the situation. If we don't know what's happening or about to happen, we become anxious and concerned and we don't like it. Remember the first day in the office when you weren't sure about the office procedures or politics. It made for a feeling of uncertainty that didn't feel good until you had learned from practice and experience what to expect.

Clients don't know what to expect on their individual matters. It is essential to explain to them what the procedures are. Here lies the benefit of the case plan and all the information you have sent them. But take time, right from the start, to explain things carefully to the client.

In particular, if you have a client who has to go to court, whether as a party to an action or a witness, go through everything that you can do to make the client feel comfortable with the situation:

- Take her to the court some time before to show her the layout of the room so that it won't come as a complete shock the day she has to give evidence.

- Tell her who the main players will be in the room and what are their functions.

- Show her who sits where.

- Advise her also on appropriate styles of dress.

- Go through with her what she will be saying to the court and pick out the strong and weak parts. Without creating too much tension, rehearse some of the points to give a flavour of the forthcoming appearance.

In America, attorneys have this element of their service down to a fine art. They get their clients to go through their testimonies in as real a court situation as they can. They will have independent advisers on what the client should wear. It is all important. For most clients, it will be much appreciated. Telling someone what to

41

expect can make a better evidence giver and help you win your case. It will also super-please the client.

RISK REVERSAL

Here is a story about two horse salesmen in the 19th Century. Both were trying to sell a pony.

One of them said to the potential buyer, "Look, Mr Smith, I think your daughter will like this pony. He's well behaved and schooled and is just the right size to suit your daughter. The pony costs £200. If, after you've had the pony for 30 days, your daughter doesn't like him then I'll take him back and you can have your money back. Now I can't say fairer than that can I?"

Sounds like a good deal. The other salesman knew about Risk Reversal.

He said, "Look Mr Smith, I think that this pony will suit your daughter down to the ground. He's well behaved and schooled. He costs £200. However he is my pony and what I suggest we do is this – pay me nothing now. I'll deliver the pony to you and stay with your daughter that afternoon to ensure that she has no immediate problems. I'll provide enough hay and feed for 30 days and arrange for him to be mucked out every morning. If, after 30 days, you don't feel that this is the right pony for your daughter, then I'll come back and take him away and you will owe me nothing. If however you feel that this is the right pony for your daughter, then you can pay me the £200 at that time."

Which pony do you think was bought?

The first deal sounded good. A money back guarantee if, after 30 days, the pony was not suitable. However, the second deal was even better. The second dealer knew about Risk Reversal.

Whenever you buy anything or use someone's services, the buyer is always taking a risk that the product or the service will be up to expectations – that it will be what he really wants. He is therefore taking a risk. If you can reverse the risk so that it falls on the seller, then the buyer is more likely to proceed to a full transaction with that seller. That is risk reversal – reversing the risk of the transaction onto the seller.

In the pony story, the risk that the father wanted to get rid of was the possibility that the pony was not suitable for his daughter after he had paid the money for it. The second dealer reversed the risk and took it upon himself. The buyer (a) didn't have to part with the purchase price, (b) did not have to meet the cost of feeding and looking after the animal for the thirty days trial period and (c) he had a guarantee that if his daughter did not like the pony for whatever reason, he could get out of the bargain and it would not cost him a penny. The risk of the transaction was totally reversed.

This is a message that sellers of legal services could well adopt and adapt.

Suppose you have someone who comes to you for a will. She finds out that your wills are £95 each. Her nearest most expensive quote is £55. She needs to be convinced that your more expensive one is the one for her.

You tell her that in addition to the will itself, she will receive an explanatory brochure detailing wills and their effect (a mini case plan specially designed by your firm), a copy of a few pages from Halsbury's Laws defining what a will is all about, and an information pack linking her will to the benefits of your financial services section.

But there is more. You need to reverse the risk of having this will. You tell her that you guarantee that she will feel 100% better that her affairs are in order after completing the will and that she does not need to pay you for it for one month.

If, after that time, she feels that she is not happy with the will you have provided for her, then she can send it back to you and she will owe you nothing. In addition, you will arrange for her to see another lawyer in a firm of her choosing to prepare another will for her. Further, that not only will she owe you nothing, you will pay for the new will to be prepared at your expense.

Now, that is a heck of a risk reversal. You have guaranteed your work and taken all the risk of the client being happy about your work on yourself. You might think that you would be daft to do something like that, but give it a go. Test it out.

See how many, if any, clients come back on the guarantee – probably not many. If you are in any case charging a respectable price for the will in the first place and giving added value to the client with the paperwork, then it should be most unlikely that you will lose out. You should have the confidence to provide this sort of guarantee and risk reversal.

If you can do it with wills, work out ways of providing a risk reversal for some of your other services.

Risk reversal is a great marketing strategy. **Insist** that your client takes you up on this service. Other lawyers in your area won't be doing it and you need to differentiate yourself in as many ways as you can. Not only that, but think about what you have done. In effect, it is only saying to your clients that you want them to be 100% happy with the service you have provided. If you personally were not happy with the service of a service provider, wouldn't you want to be able to get your money back? Under these circumstances, you must have a super-pleased client. Think what she's got:

- a professionally prepared will

- added value in terms of a specially prepared explanatory brochure or case plan

- Halsbury's Laws extract

- a guarantee that if she doesn't like the will, she can get another free of charge

- she doesn't have to pay unless she is 100% happy about the will

- a link into your financial services section so that you can start cross selling some financial products.

It all adds up to a super-pleased client.

THE NEW BUSINESS CO-ORDINATOR (NBC)

When someone new rings or comes into the office, a system **must** be in place to deal with the inquirer **immediately.** It is important to give the newcomer to the firm the right impression. Having the receptionist wander round the office desperately trying to find someone who will see this person is no good at all. The newcomer must be regarded as good news and not as an interruption to the day. That is why you must have someone who is able to deal with new business, continually on standby.

This person must be specially trained in marketing and listening skills and be personable enough to get new business, and must therefore be allowed time off his or her fee-earning capability to do this important job. Also, your new business co-ordinator needs backup from the rest of the office.

If the NBC sees someone who needs matrimonial advice, he or she needs to direct that person to the matrimonial experts in your office. The NBC should be showing new clients to their new legal advisers after the initial interview has been completed.

There should be a new client information form to complete and a copy should be given to the new adviser as well as the accounts/computer section. As many details as possible about the client's situation need to be completed and then the new client can be re-directed to the appropriate lawyer.

The potential client who comes in for a conveyancing quote or a quote of any kind **must** be dealt with by the same person who then has the opportunity to 'sell' the firm and pass the client on to the appropriate lawyer. Your NBC has a vital job to do in grabbing that business. If a potential client comes through the door asking for a quote, the NBC should be able to secure that business and **not** let it go away to another firm to 'compare quotes'. He or she should be sufficiently persuasive and be able to show that your firm is the right one for that client.

The potential client who telephones for a quote on conveyancing or indeed any other matter, should also be put through to the new business co-ordinator. The task then is to secure that business.

How? The first task is to get the client into the office. Then there is a much better chance, if not an outright certainty, of getting the business. Maybe the conversation might go as follows:

Quote getter: It's Alan Potter here. I'm ringing for a quote on conveyancing. I'm buying a house for £120,000 and need a £60,000 mortgage. I've got no house to sell. How much will you charge me? *(Resist the temptation to tell him what he wants.)*

New Business Co-ordinator (NBC): "Hello Mr Potter. Thanks for calling. Could I ask you one or two questions?"

Potter: "Yes."

NBC: "Have you already arranged a mortgage for your new home through an Independent Financial Adviser or a lender with a tie into a particular source?"

Potter: "I've had a quote from one source. He said he could only quote on one Company's Mortgage so I am looking around to see what other people do."

NBC: "Yes, I can understand why you would want to look round. *(Agreeing with him)* Tell me, Mr Potter, are you looking for a really low-cost mortgage or one that has maximum benefits for you?"

Potter: "Well, I don't want to pay over the odds, but I'm really looking for a mortgage linked to a policy that will provide a sort of savings plan as well."

NBC: "Great. That sounds like a good idea. At the office here we run a totally Independent Financial advice section that can give you that type of advice."

Potter: "Oh, right."

NBC: "Mr Potter, did anyone mention that commission is payable if you take on a new policy?"

Potter: "No."

NBC: "Well, the insurance company that supply the policy will pay commission to the adviser who arranges the policy. Because we are solicitors, we are bound to tell you that the commission is yours to keep."

Potter: "That sounds good. But what do you get out of it. You're not doing all that work for free."

NBC: "No, you're right, Mr Potter. We would give you an account for half of the total commission for the work in advising you on the best policy for you."

Potter: "Sounds good. But what about the legal costs?"

NBC: "I'd love to give you a quote which will be fixed no matter what. Can I ask you to come to the office to go through it with me?"

Potter: "Can't you tell me now?"

NBC: "We have a policy of not quoting on the telephone just in case there are any misunderstandings. I would like to meet you and give you the quote here and let you have one of our information packs which contains details of other ways that you can save money in the moving process. I can be available to see you immediately. Can you come now or would it be better to see you sometime tomorrow?"

Potter: "Umm ... I've got to collect my wife from work. Can I bring her along and see you in an hour's time?"

NBC: "That's fine. Do you know where we are?"

Potter: "Yes. I'll see you then."

NBC: "Thanks, Mr Potter. I'll wait for you." *(showing him that he is important enough already to have his lawyer waiting for him.)*

If the caller says that he can't see you straight away then say,

"Fine, I can appreciate that you may be busy at the moment. Could you come to see me at 10am tomorrow or would sometime on Thursday be better?"

Give the caller a choice – then he's thinking about **when** he can see you, not **whether** to see you. If the caller says that he just can't get to see you say,

> "Fine, I can understand that, Mr Potter. *(People like people who understand them)* I think it is so important that you get independent advice about your new mortgage because, after all, it is going to be with you for many years to come. I think it is so important that I would be willing to see you and your wife at home to discuss your requirements further. Would it be possible to see you tonight at 6pm or sometime on Thursday evening?"

If he is still objecting to this, you probably have one of the employees of another law firm on the other end of the phone, who is ringing up to find out how much you charge so that he can relate it to his boss!

The new business co-ordinator is in a unique position to see what other services the client may want. The answers to the questions should switch on lights about the various services that can be offered by the firm. Pay the person well – the NBC should be an excellent source of new work to the firm if the job is done properly. You can monitor this by checking each month to see precisely what has resulted from his or her activities. The NBC should be reporting to a Partner and discussing what's going on so that trends can be spotted early.

The new business co-ordinator should always, always, always ask new potential client why they have chosen your particular firm.

- Was it by **recommendation?** If so, from whom? Tell new clients that you have a policy of writing to thank the people who recommended them to the firm – if it is all right with them.

- You need to know if new clients have come to you as a result of an **advertisement** you have produced – if so, precisely which one so that you can monitor the adverts that you publish to check their efficiency.

- Did they just come in after seeing your **nameplate**?

- Was something in your **literature** attractive to them and if so, what?

- Were they looking for a lawyer in **Yellow Pages** and saw your advert. If that is the case, why did they choose you over the other firms listed there?

You must get to the bottom of why you were chosen. It will help with your future marketing. You must know what works.

Remember that your new business co-ordinator deals with the new clients who come into the office off the street or by phone. But it is the job of **everybody** in the office to seek new work and introduce it to the office. All staff must know this and appreciate that this is part of their employment.

WHAT ELSE NEEDS LOOKING AT?

THE MAIL ROOM

It is vital that you arrange for your post arriving in the office to be opened and distributed as quickly as possible. Don't wait for the Post Office to deliver. You are at the mercy of the postman and, if he decides to stop off for a cup of coffee one day, then your post will be that much later. You simply must have it in your office first thing and deal with it. Arrange with the Post Office that you will collect the mail personally and then make sure that it is collected as soon as you can each morning.

A partner must supervise the opening of the mail.

Most of the problems that come into a lawyer's office come via the mail. Any complaint letters from clients, any nasty letters from the Law Society or Office for the Supervision of Solicitors will then be apparent. It is then that you can deal with anything that is a problem and you must deal with it straight away. Do not leave it for the employee concerned to sort out. He will probably need help even if he doesn't ask for it. If the problem is not sorted straight away, then you will be bubbling up larger problems for the future. There is little worse than having a negligence action against the firm. Not only is it bad news for the firm but it takes up so much unproductive time – time that you cannot afford to lose. So supervise the opening of post and deal with all problems immediately.

THE CASE PLAN

Every reasonably major piece of work for a client should have a case or transaction plan. In fact, with the universal availability of word processors, there is no reason why **every** job shouldn't have a case plan. It should be graphically designed specifically for the firm and it should look professional. It should contain the following:

- **details of the problem that your client has told you**

- **the procedure that you will adopt to solve the problem**

- **what the client needs to do**

- **costings**

- **description of any major document that is likely to be forthcoming with an explanation of what terms mean**

- **a copy of the representation agreement.**

If you take on a client who wants a will, you may think that a case plan is not necessary. However, you must develop the habit of thinking 'added value for the client'. Give him an A4 sheet of paper, nicely laid out with the firm's name on it, which briefly explains what a will is for, some information about Inheritance Tax and how the thing can be made invalid – also, when to review it.

You need only create the page once as it will be suitable for most of the clients you prepare wills for. It is also a piece of paper that your client will cherish. He will brag about it to his friends when the topic comes up. 'My lawyer sent me a case plan with loads of extra information about wills – it was great.'

Send the client paper.

Super-please him.

COMPLAINTS BY CLIENTS

The Office for the Supervision of Solicitors

Think about this – why on earth should solicitors need an organisation like this? It started life as the Solicitors' Complaints Bureau which of itself was **bad, bad** news. For the Law Society, as the Solicitors' professional governing body, to even **think** of a name which emphasises complaints about solicitors is bad news. To set up a whole bureaucracy clearly implies and advertises the fact that there are thousands of complaints (which there are) and as a result of having the office, so business will be generated. As you attract, so you will receive. If you have a body to deal specifically with complaints, then they will emerge, no matter what.

Now we have the Office for the Supervision of Solicitors. Do solicitors need 'supervision'? What are they talking about? It is a disgrace to the profession to think that this office just deals with the problems that are caused by solicitors.

Your actions over complaints

You need to ensure that your procedures in the office are sufficient to handle any problems without having an outside 'supervision' body to pick up this unwanted baggage. You must treat a complaint not as a problem but as an opportunity to super-delight the client with what you **can** do.

If you really have fouled up, then admit it. Admit it quickly and negotiate a solution. This will work for 95% of such problems. However, if it is a negligence claim, then you **must** cease acting for the client and tell him he must instruct another lawyer to get **independent** advice. Do all you can to cooperate with that lawyer and try to sort out a settlement. Notify the Solicitors Indemnity Fund. But if it is within your excess, you will be paying the compensation anyway.

The secret is to make absolutely sure that it is settled as **quickly** as possible. Why?

- It will save you the hassle of dealing with the problem if it drags on.

- You might actually keep the client if he sees you handle the complaint quickly and efficiently. He may see that it was just an unusual hitch and that generally he likes and trusts you.

- If it goes on, then you will be repeatedly dealing with it instead of getting stuck into productive work that you like.

- It is a real pain if the complaint stays in your filing cabinet. Every time you look at it, your heart will sink and you won't like it.

- Your client will tell family and friends that the problem was sorted quickly.

Consider the activities of one American firm. They give a **guarantee** with their work about complaints. When they have a complaint against them from a client, if that individual or organisation is not satisfied within **four hours** that the matter is resolved to their complete satisfaction, then **all of the client's bill for that matter is wiped out – regardless of how much that might be!**

Now that is a very bold guarantee. How many of us would be willing to stick our necks out that far? If we wouldn't be so willing, then **why not**?

So, insist that your complaint handling procedures are working efficiently. **Do not** actually call it a 'Complaints Procedure' – call it something else, a 'Quality Check' or 'Client Query Procedure'. Present a positive air about it. Nobody likes to talk about 'complaints'.

WHAT IS IN YOUR WINDOW?

Why is it that lawyers have the most appalling things in their windows? At this very moment, there are lawyers' windows full of old adding and calculator machines, wooden dolls houses, old tin toy cars and the favourite piece of bric-a-brac seems to be the quill pen, ink pot and the set of scales. Very Dickensian. Why, for goodness' sake, do lawyers clutter their windows with this rubbish? What does it say to the potential client? Certainly nothing about the efficient way the firm is run or the standard of advice lawyers give or the range of services on offer.

What it says is ... 'I can't think what on earth to put in this window so I'll shove in some stuff that I bought at an auction, that has a really vague legal connection and leave it there for a few years.'

Get that rubbish out of your windows, especially if you have ground-floor, shopfront accommodation. You must make the window work for you. Have a look at the financial institutions who have spent thousands on their windows. Take a leaf out of their books and get something designed to reflect the professional aspect of your business. It does not have to be boring but it should be eye-catching.

In these days of super graphics and multi-media wizardry, a plain and tatty window display does absolutely nothing to encourage new people to call in for advice. Move with the times, but compatible with the legal business and present to the public something that attracts and invites.

Get a graphic designer to design a window display to attract new clients and replace it regularly. If you know people in the theatre or in retail sales, ask them for ideas - they know the value of making things visually attractive. It does not have to be hugely expensive, but it must attract potential clients and it must reflect your approach and philosophy.

One easy thing you can do today – tear down those brown and faded Legal Aid stickers. They say so much about your firm and it is all negative.

HOW TO SELL PAPERS TO CLIENTS THAT THEY WILL LOVE

The trouble with the work that lawyers do is that it is intangible. You cannot touch it. You get nothing for your money that you can actually pass from hand to hand. So the more tangible you can make your practice, the better the client will be able to understand and appreciate it.

That is why we have talked about information packs, brochures, leaflets and case plans that you give or send to your clients. They all reinforce the tangibility of your service for your clients and they feel that they are receiving something for their money. They do not **really** understand that they are actually paying for advice. So the answer is to couple the advice with paperwork.

Suppose one of your clients (not a voice at the end of the telephone, but an established client) asks you about his purchase of a £10,000 second-hand car. He has just bought it and the thing isn't working properly. In fact it isn't working at all after just three days. He has seen another car for the same price from a different garage and wants to know as a matter of urgency if he can escape from the first contract, sling the car back and get a full refund so that he can secure the second car, which will be sold elsewhere that afternoon unless he agrees to buy it.

He needs advice that is up to date and he needs it straight away. You give it to him over the telephone. He is grateful and returns to the first garage, retrieves his money and buys the second car, which turns out to be the one he has always wanted.

Now, suppose you send him an account that bills him '£30 for the telephone call'. He won't like it and will think that it is a very expensive phone call. This takes us back to the idea that legal services are completely intangible and somewhat ethereal in the minds of the paying public. You need to present your client with real evidence that you have earned your fee and that you do really know what you are talking about. So, send him a bill that explains all this and accompany it with some relevant papers that help to explain the law. Something like this:

TO OUR PROFESSIONAL CHARGES for advising you
on the 5th October 200-, in respect of the contract you
had entered into for the purchase of a car including
advising you on Sections 12-15 of the Sale of Goods
Act 1979 and Section 6 of the Unfair Contract Terms
Act 1977 and the problems you were experiencing in
respect of the fitness and merchantability of the car and
advising you of your right to rescind the initial contract
and negotiate the return of your monies –

£120.00

You then write to him **on the same day** with a letter confirming the advice you gave over the telephone. You enclose your bill in the letter. In addition, you send him copies of the appropriate sections of the Acts which you have referred to and a couple of pages from Halsbury's Laws on the Sale of Goods. That way, you've added value to your advice.

He is more likely to be happy to pay the larger amount because he will feel that he got something tangible for the money and you have caught him at a time when he is still pleased about the actual outcome.

He will also think that he has a lawyer who is on the ball and able to deal with this sort of problem and that will make him **feel** good.

So far as you are concerned, you will have done the following:

- super-pleased your client

- increased your income four times over and above what you dreaded it would be for that piece of advice over the phone

- made a written record of the advice for future use thus ensuring that there is some documentary evidence of your advice in case there is any later query

- sent out your bill at the optimum time according to the Client's Curve of Gratitude (see later)

- added value to your advice.

'THANK YOU' LETTERS AND CARDS

Saying 'thank you' to someone is so much appreciated – more so if it comes from a professional person, and even more so again, if it comes from one's lawyer.

Many lawyers do not ask new clients if they were recommended by some other person. Nor do they send a letter thanking that person for the introduction. Develop the habit of asking where the new client has found out about the firm. If the idea came by way of a personal recommendation, then for goodness' sake thank the person who sent the new client. If possible, telephone him or her. Then back it up with a letter along these lines:

ABC SOLICITORS

Dear Joe,

Very many thanks for recommending Alan Potter to me.

Although you will appreciate that for confidential reasons I cannot let you know the outcome of the meeting, I am grateful to you for your suggestion that he contact me.

You may know that most of my work comes from recommendations by existing clients and I much appreciate your taking the time to recommend Alan to me.

Best wishes.

Yours sincerely,

CHRISTMAS CARDS

One wonderful way to keep in touch with your clients is to send them Christmas Cards every year. **But** do not get a cheap box from Woollies and send them one of those. Put some time and effort into it. Remember it is something else – something tangible – that is coming from your firm. It is an advert from the firm and should follow the same rules as everything else from the firm in terms of its presentation.

Arrange to purchase (or have printed) a card that is specially designed every year. If you chose a good graphic designer and give him the brief each year, he should be able to come up with some really good and interesting designs that will be unique to your firm. Then send a card to **every** client and **every** contact and referral source you have.

Make sure you sign them personally and if possible write a short personal note on each one. You may not think you have time to do this in December, so get the cards printed in early November so you will have plenty of time to write messages on each card and sign them.

BIRTHDAY CARDS

You need to develop the idea that the client is a friend. Sending birthday cards should be usual for a friend. If your computer is good enough, you should be able to produce a list of clients' birthdays each day so that you can send out the appropriate cards. As with the Christmas cards, arrange to have some specially designed each year for the firm.

THE VOICE ON THE END OF THE TELEPHONE

The very **last** person you want to be giving advice to is the new, anonymous voice at the end of the phone. He is **not** a client. You do **not** know him. It is always urgent. He only wants a few minutes of your time – and he won't hold you to what you say. Do **not** be caught out by this caller. Tell him that you do **not under any circumstances** give advice to non-clients over the telephone. Tell him you understand that it is urgent. Tell him that you will drop everything and be available in the office immediately to see him.

If he really is genuine, then he will respond to your invitation and you can start a new relationship with a new client. If he doesn't want to come to the office or more probably just doesn't show up, then forget him. You were never going to get him as a new client in the first place.

Furthermore, you will have cut down your chance of being sued in six months' time for negligent advice because this voice never actually told you the full story in those few brief moments on the phone. Remember you know nothing about him and giving advice over the telephone to non-clients is a very dangerous move. You will have nothing to back up what you said even if you can remember the call.

IMAGE

This is something that most lawyers ignore. However, they now do so at their peril. Image covers everything from the firm's biros to the senior partners' boardroom, from the style and quality of the stationery to the way the receptionists dress.

There are a few basics that you need to sort out as a priority. They are the ones that the public and clients see regularly.

First of all is your paperwork. This means every piece of paper that comes out of the office. It includes the letterheads, bills, brochures, 'With Compliments' slips, leaflets, Christmas cards, information packs, continuation sheets – everything – the lot that has taken a tree or two to produce for you. Look at them, have a really good look at them and ask yourself these two questions:

1   When were they last reviewed?

2   Could they be improved with professional help?

For most firms, the last review was in the Dark Ages. The senior partner thought it a great idea to have a quill pen and ink bottle on the letterhead and nobody has thought to question it since. Well, seize the time **now** and get a graphic designer to help you. Do **not** do it yourself. You will just end up with the up-to-date version of the quill pen.

The letterhead and all the firm's material must have a common theme. There must be no doubt that the piece of paper that is being scanned is from your firm. They must be **recognisably** yours.

They must all be designed with this common theme in mind. One firm has chosen a prowling orange cat as its logo. It is unique and that is what you are trying to produce – something that differentiates you from all the other lawyers. You do not actually **need** a fancy or cunning logo. Clifford Chance, the largest law firm in the world, do not have a logo, but they do have a **very characteristic typeface** that was designed specially for them and is used on all their documentation. In addition, they use a quality of paper that is not normally used by lawyers.

So start with the paperwork. But remember that **image** does not stop there. It includes the whole look of the office, including the lettering on the glass and the display in the window. Many firms bought the Legal Aid logo sticker when it was first introduced and that is still on display in many windows. It is faded, discoloured and peeling and looks absolutely awful. Get it off the window and in the bin – now! And get cracking on jetting your image into the 21st Century – after all, we are there already!

The reception area is one place which is approached by virtually all of the firm's clients, whether they are new or old-established. Give a tremendous amount of thought to the look of the room. What's in it? Why?

If it still houses a wilting yucca plant and 1970s copies of Punch, then it is high time for a revamp. Get some professional help for the design of the room. It is all important because it is the first place that the potential client goes to. The first impression for the client off the street is the waiting area and it has to match the image you want to portray of the firm, whatever that may be.

The reception area must also be a suitable place for your professional clients to assemble or wait – they will expect a similar degree of style and functionality to their own premises. This of course depends on the type of service that you are providing. Remember the phrase 'people like people who are like they are'. If your main target groups of clients are the international, multi-faceted conglomerates, then you will need style, scale and pizazz to match.

AN IN-DEPTH LOOK AT BILLING

In this section, we are going to take a look at billing in non-contentious matters. The firm's income derives mostly from the bills that it produces, so it is **absolutely vital** that your billing is correct. There is little point in running a legal office if your billing procedure loses money every time you produce a bill.

WHAT SHOULD BE PUT IN THE BILL ITSELF?

We have a tendency to think that, since we have done the work, we should be entitled to be paid for the work. It should not be something we have to justify to the client. However, that is a wrong assumption. A lot of the work that is done by the lawyer is not known about by the client. Consequently the bill is the time to explain the things to him that you have done. Include a reference to all documents which you have worked on. It is a good practice to be preparing the narrative to the bill as you work. Keep it on the computer and update it as you go. This will ensure that by the time you come to prepare the actual bill, you are ready to send it out immediately. Never let there be a delay in sending the bill because you haven't got the time to prepare it – do it in advance.

Never detail the disbursements on your bill. The client looks at the total amount and thinks that it is all going to you. Put a list of the disbursements on a separate Statement of Account.

WHEN SHOULD THE BILL BE SUBMITTED?

The example about the dud car should give you the clue that you submit your bill of costs at the **earliest possible moment** after you have finished the work. Clients will be happier to pay a bill immediately because they will still have the service you provided fresh in their minds. If you leave it for a month, the incentive to pay wanes. (See the Client's Curve of Gratitude)

SHOULD THE BILL BE A NARRATIVE ONE OR A SHORT ONE?

Which of the following bills would you be happy to pay?

Bill Number 1

> TO OUR PROFESSIONAL CHARGES for acting on your behalf in relation to your dispute
>
> £1250.00

Bill Number 2

> TO OUR PROFESSIONAL CHARGES incurred in connection with acting on your behalf in relation to your dispute with the Manager at Car U Like and including all correspondence and phone calls
>
> £1250.00

Bill Number 3

> TO OUR PROFESSIONAL CHARGES incurred in connection with acting on your behalf in relation to your dispute with the Manager of Car U Like concerning your car purchased on 3rd March 200- receiving instructions from you by telephone; attending at the

office of Car U Like that afternoon with you but being unable to negotiate a settlement at that time; locating and telephoning Car U Like's General Manager to explain the position to him; faxing copies of the correspondence to him and subsequently attending at the local offices of the Company with you to negotiate a final settlement; preparing the terms of the Settlement Document and obtaining the approval of the Solicitors for the Company of the terms; attending the office of Car U Like and agreeing the final points in the Settlement Agreement with you subsequently preparing the final version and attending with you at the London offices of the Company to finalise the arrangement and collect a cheque in your favour for £15,899. (Services rendered on 2, 3, 4, 5, 6, 7, 8, 10, 11, 12, 13, 14, 15, 16, 19, 20, 23, 25, 26, 28 March 200-)
Thank you   £1250.00

Which of the above bills would you prefer to pay? Be sure to give the client information about what you have done for him.

HOW TO BILL FRIENDS AND RELATIVES AND ANYONE ELSE WHO YOU WANT TO GIVE A DISCOUNT TO

Friends and relatives should be a good source of work for your business. They do however have two inherent problems:

- they don't think that they should have to pay full whack for your services
- they have no idea how much you normally charge for a particular job.

If you are happy to give them a discount on your normal fees, you must tell them how much of a discount you have given them. The bill should read:

.....and advising you on the final Loan Document prior to attending upon you for signature. (Services rendered on 2, 3, 5, 6, 8, 9 and 10 March 200-)

Normal Charge	£450.00
Less Family Discount	£200.00
Balance Payable:	£250.00

Thank you

THE COST OF RUNNING THE FIRM

Each firm should work out their expense rate for each forthcoming year. That is the cost of actually running the firm but excluding any profit element – in other words, the costs of just keeping the doors open. Then divide that total cost – the expense rate – by 12 to give the monthly cost of running the firm. Seek advice from a competent accountant who is used to dealing with solicitors' accounts to help you complete this exercise for the first time. Thereafter, you should be able to manage it yourself. Also, The Law Society's *Expense of Time* booklet will assist in this process.

A budget can then be prepared on an annual, in-advance basis. The figure can include the profit element you hope to make in the year and this figure divided by 12 will give you the monthly income you expect to make. That can then be divided into the number of fee earners, albeit not on an equal basis, and you then have a monthly target figure to monitor for each fee earner. It is not an **exact** method because it does not take into account, for example, seasonal variations. However, it is possible to monitor this each month to see how the fee-earners are doing. Any great discrepancy will then be revealed and appropriate action can be taken.

TIME RECORDING

Most lawyer's work needs to be logged properly. There are a number of computerised systems that can help you do this. But for whatever system you use, whether a manual or a computerised system, you will have to get used to the fact that time recording is a **pain.**

Some lawyers advocate that you should only record the time you are actually working on client matters. However, you **should record the whole day**. This would then include time you spend researching, being involved on marketing matters, entertaining, and other non billable matters. Then you will have some idea as to what your firm is doing. If, for example, one of the partners is spending a quarter of her time on marketing matters, you are then in a position to work out whether you consider that to be a good use of her time or whether it should be done by someone else.

Also there is a school of thought that argues that if standard fixed price work is being done – conveyancing, for example – where a fixed quote has been given, then there is no point to time recording. That is nonsense. You may well decide to have fixed cost work and there is nothing wrong with fixed cost (as opposed to **low** cost). However, you still need to monitor how much it is costing you to produce that work. If one of the lawyers is spending continually more time than is profitable to produce a certain type of work, then you need to check this and either increase the cost, get someone more junior to deal with it or drop the work entirely. All these judgements can only be made if you have a decent time recording system in place. Remember you are keeping time records, **not** billing records. The time records are only an aid to billing and do not replace the whole billing process.

Time sheets are simple to produce and duplicate. They should show the full working day divided into units of time – use units of six minutes – and must have a facility for recording which matter is being dealt with for each time unit. Then introduce the record sheets, advising all the staff to take into account that all the day's time has to be allocated and that the particular matter being dealt with needs to be identified. Devise special codes for the activities that will be recorded. For example, T for telephone calls and L for letters. At the end of each day, the time sheets of everybody in the office go to the accounts department who will then update the computer records for each client matter.

As this might be quite a cultural change for your firm, the

introduction of time-sheets needs to be handled with a degree of diplomacy and by seeking agreement on the benefits to be derived from them.

TIME RECORDING IS AN AID TO BILLING

When you come to prepare a bill, the time records become all important. It must be remembered that they are only an **aid** to preparing the bill. The other factors contained in the *Solicitors' (Non-Contentious Business) Remuneration Order 1994* need to be looked at as well (for non-contentious work).

BILLING – LET'S GO DEEPER!

Most of the firm's income comes from the bills it produces. It is **essential** therefore that your billing is as good as you can make it.

Let us take a look at non-contentious costs.

Section 87 of the Solicitors Act 1974 defines Non-contentious business as *'any business done as a solicitor which is not contentious business'* – an excellent bit of lawyer-talk!

We need to know what contentious business is to interpret that definition. Contentious business is *'business done whether as solicitor or advocate in or for the purposes of proceedings begun before a court or before an arbitrator appointed under the Arbitration Act 1950 other than non-contentious or probate business.'*

So non-contentious work therefore includes the following:

- conveyancing
- probate
- administration of estates
- trusts
- wills
- planning applications

- licensing
- all work done preliminary to court proceedings in contentious matters if such proceedings are **not** subsequently begun.

The Solicitors' (Non-Contentious Business) Remuneration Order 1994 ('the Order') is the Statutory provision which deals with these types of costs.

Article 3 of the Order states that the Solicitor's remuneration for non-contentious work *'shall be such sum as may be fair and reasonable to both the solicitor and the entitled person having regard to all the circumstances of the case and in particular to:*

(1) the complexity of the matter or the difficulty or novelty of the questions raised (the <u>complexity</u> factor)

(2) the skill, labour, specialised knowledge and responsibility involved (the <u>skill</u> factor)

(3) the time spent on the business (the <u>time</u> factor)

(4) the number and importance of the documents prepared or perused, without regard to length (the <u>documents</u> factor)

(5) the place where and the circumstances in which the business or any part thereof is transacted (the <u>place</u> factor)

(6) the amount or value of any money or property involved (the <u>value</u> factor)

(7) whether any land involved is registered land (the <u>title</u> factor)

(8) the importance of the matter to the client (the <u>importance</u> factor)

(9) the approval (express or implied) of the entitled person or the express approval of the testator to:

> *(i) the solicitor undertaking all or any part of the work giving rise to the costs; or*
> *(ii) the amount of the costs'* (the <u>approval</u> factor)

These Factors in the Order are the matters which you have to consider when preparing any bill.

HOW TO WORK OUT THE CORRECT AMOUNT TO BILL

The calculation of the correct amount to charge a client is an exercise in judgment. It is **not** solely an arithmetical one. Your time sheet will help to show how much time has been spent on the matter (Factor 3 above). However this is only one of the factors to be taken into account.

Some basic workings need to be done before you can prepare any bill of costs. You need to know:

1   What is the cost of doing the work?
2   What is the profit element to be added to the bill?

The *Expense of Time* booklet and procedure for working out the firm's accounts are therefore useful. The Law Society also publish guidelines on mark-ups or profit elements.

These factors are also important to note:

* Record everything – a file note **and** a time sheet entry are both needed.

* Record not only attendances, but also perusal and preparation time.

* Time spent considering law and procedure is not chargeable unless the case is unusual or infrequent.

Once the foundation is laid for successful billing, then individual bills can be looked at. The starting point is to decide whether you have a routine matter or a non-routine matter.

1. Non-routine cases

If it is non-routine, then the procedure is as follows:

1 **The Broad Look**
First take a broad look at all the circumstances of the case. Have a look at the file and see if any one of the Article 3 factors dwarfs the others. For example, the value factor if the matter relates to a £3 million sale.

2 **The Other Factors**
Next consider all the other factors in Article 3. Consider to what extent the factors of complexity, skill, time, documents, place, value, title, importance and approval are apparent.

3 **The Adrenalin Factor**
Then consider if this element – the adrenalin factor – (which is not one of the Article 3 elements) plays a part. Donaldson J (as he then was) introduced this element in *Treasury Solicitor v Register (1978) 2 All ER 920.* You need to ask – did the lawyer have to work very fast with little or no margin for error? If he did, then the final bill must be increased to take this into account.

4 **Check the Law Society Guidelines**
In the Law Society's *An Approach to Non-Contentious Costs*, the Society recommend percentage charging in bands where high value transactions are involved.

5 **Calculation**
Make a judgment as to whether you consider the sum to be fair and reasonable, based on the above.

6 **Bill Approval Form and Review**

Complete the bill approval form (see later) and get it reviewed by another lawyer in the firm.

2. Routine cases

1 **The Broad Look**

Take a look at all the circumstances of the case and review the file.

2 **Time Records**

Check the time records for that particular matter.

3 **Value Factor**

(a) If there is a value element, then check the Law Society's *An Approach to Non-Contentious Costs* Booklet. It specifically refers to percentage mark-ups on domestic conveyancing, leases, mortgages and probates.

(b) If there is no value factor, then the costs will be the hourly cost of doing the work extracted from your time sheet records together with a mark-up. The mark-up will usually be 50% but can be more or less depending on the circumstances of the case and how the other factors in Article 3 have a bearing.

4 **Calculation**

Add the chargeable time sum to the mark-up figure. Then look at the final sum and make a judgment as to whether this is considered to be a fair and reasonable sum.

5 **Bill Approval Form and Review**

Complete the bill approval form and get it reviewed by another lawyer in the firm.

HOW TO DEAL WITH OVERTIME

Overtime often presents enormous difficulties. If you have worked overtime for a client who **requires** that you work quickly, then you can charge him extra. However, if you do work out of office hours because this suits your way of working, then this is not something that you can charge extra for.

If you are genuinely working for the client at night or the weekends, then find some reason to telephone the client at home. He will appreciate that you are working for him out of office hours.

DISLOCATION

Dislocation covers time spent on a client's matter outside normal office hours solely in order to fulfil the needs or requirements of a client. As a consequence, you can charge more for this element. For example, a client may ring you in the evening and say that he is setting off for a trip abroad and is worried that he hasn't got a will. He is desperate to get one sorted there and then, so you visit the client to advise on a will and prepare a hand-written one on the spot. You are entitled to charge more for this type of work.

TRAVELLING TIME

All travelling time should be recorded and charged to the client on whose behalf the journey is being made unless it has been possible to do other work during the journey which can be charged for.

TEAMWORK

It is often the case that more than one person has been dealing with a particular matter. That other person's time should be included in the calculation when the bill is prepared. The time sheet should be designed to allow for other people to be working on a particular file to record that involvement. If a lawyer checks a point with a colleague then the colleague simply includes that discussion on his time sheet including the file reference number of the enquiring lawyer.

TELEPHONE CALLS

Long telephone calls where advice is given to the client or where matters are taken further can be charged for. In other words, when something of substance is done or discussed, it can be included on the time sheet just like an attendance. *Bwanaoga v Bwanaoga (1979) 2 All ER 105* confirms that this is the case.

SPECIALISTS

If you are a specialist practising in the Provinces, then you can use a higher hourly rate figure than that regarded as the norm for your area. *(Jones and Another v Secretary of State and Another)* The Times, 3rd December 1996.

THE BILL APPROVAL FORM

In all cases, when it is time to prepare the bill of costs, a bill approval form should be completed by the lawyer who has done the work. This will give a breakdown of the work actually undertaken. The bills approval form is a document prepared and designed for the firm by a graphic designer with knowledge of legal firms. It should include the following:

• broad look comments

• any monetary figure

- if it involved property, whether the title was registered or unregistered

- whether a mortgage has been arranged for the client if so, details

- whether an insurance policy has been arranged for the client and if so, how the commission was dealt with and the amount of the commission

- the amount of time units to date

- the amount of expected additional time units to conclusion

- details of any person who referred the client to the firm

- comments on:

  - complexity
  - dislocation
  - number of documents
  - expertise or skill
  - number of long distance phone calls
  - where the work was undertaken if not in the office
  - importance to the client
  - adrenalin factor

- whether the client has introduced any work to the firm

- whether the client has produced other work for the firm

- whether the client should be seen/telephoned before the bill is sent

- suggested charge by the lawyer who actually did the work

- any additional comments by the lawyer who did the work.

WHO SHOULD PREPARE THE BILL?

This item of activity must be completed by:

(a) the lawyer who has done the work, **and**
(b) another lawyer who oversees the first lawyer's work who looks at the file with the bill approval form.

The lawyer who has done the work should prepare the bill in draft with the help of the Accounts Department. He or she should look at the family photo on the side desk whilst doing the bill and keep firmly in mind that it is his or her income that provides all the benefits for the family. It shouldn't make any difference – but it does! Then the first lawyer should liaise with the second lawyer about precisely how much the bill should be. There is a tendency for the lawyer who actually does the work to under-bill. This is negated by the objective look by the other lawyer. Then the first lawyer can present any arguments that there are about the client and whether a full bill should or should not be produced.

Remember though that if you decide to give a genuine discount, let the client know. See the item (page 65) about billing friends and anyone else who **you** think deserves a discount. If you do not tell them that they are getting a discount they will never know.

THE CLIENTS' CURVE OF GRATITUDE

The Clients' Curve of Gratitude is simply and solely designed to reinforce the idea that you should prepare your bill as soon as you have finished the work. The client very quickly forgets how brilliant you were and if you leave it a month or two, or even a week or two, to send your bill to the client, it will be resented and the client who was delighted with your services on the day things were settled will object to the amount and possibly even to getting a bill at all. Have it ready to send – and send it – at the earliest possible moment. But first go through the procedure about preparing the bill referred to earlier.

It is essential that you are being paid the correct amount for the work you have done.

8 DAY OF SETTLEMENT
"What a great lawyer. I owe him everything – my business, my career – I'd recommend him to anyone."

7 ON THE COURT STEPS
"You did it! I don't know how – I think I'm dreaming! I'll send a cheque to the other side right now."

9 TEN DAYS LATER
"He's a great lawyer and he did a great job, but the law and the facts were on my side."

6 AFTER CONTRACT IS NON-ADMISSIBLE
"You've got them worried – try to settle it.

10 THREE WEEKS LATER
"He's a pretty good lawyer, but I think that the judge would have decided in my favour."

5 AT COURT
"Do you really think that you can get that damaging contract thrown out of court?"

11 ONE MONTH LATER
"He did his job, but there was no way I could lose."

4 AFTER TWO WEEKS OF AFFIDAVITS FROM THE OTHER SIDE
"You really must have worked hard to know so much about the car engine."

12 SIX WEEKS LATER
"I never needed a lawyer to begin with. He made a big case out of a small problem."

3 TWO DAYS LATER – FIRST MEETING WITH SOLICITOR
"If I lose, I'm bankrupt!"

13 TEN WEEKS LATER
"He must think I am daft if he thinks that I'm paying this bill!"

2 NEXT DAY
"It's even worse – I'd forgotten that I have cancelled my negligence insurance policy!"

14 THREE MONTHS LATER
"That shark! He's sued me! I am reporting him to the Law Society AND starting a claim for professional negligence!"

1 WRIT SERVED ON CLIENT
"Help! I'm in big trouble! I should never have sold that car without checking it. I did not know that it was defective and got involved in a multi-car smash!"

THE CLIENT'S CURVE OF GRATITUDE
(adapted from an original idea by American Attorney Jay G Foonberg)

The optimum time for sending your bill is between points 8 and 9

AGREEING FEES

The last thing that a lawyer wants to do when he gets to work is to talk to a new client about his fee. He is usually embarrassed about having to talk about money! It is perhaps no surprise. For generations, lawyers just billed their clients without discussing how much the fee would be. Even now, barristers do not discuss the subject at all. Their clerks do the negotiating about fees. However, now solicitors must be able to discuss fees without any embarrassment. Lawyers negotiate a great deal on behalf of clients and it is these skills that need to be used when agreeing fees with clients. If you feel that your negotiating skills are not good, then join a negotiating course. It is important to remember that both you and the client have to be happy at the end of the negotiations and that the agreed fee is acceptable to both you and the client.

Here are a few tips:

- Be firm. When you're talking about money, be confident and firm. If you are uncertain or lack confidence, the client will pick this up and seek reductions.

- **Do not** ask the client what he thinks the fee should be. This is a disastrous move. If the client thinks that he can assess your fee, he will lose all confidence in you.

- Don't change your mind. Once you've agreed a fee, stick to it. If you then try to change the fee, the client will think that you were deliberately trying to overcharge him in the first place.

- Don't lower your fee to bring it in line or below another quote that the client has received. If the client tells you what the other quote is, then use this to your advantage. Get the client to look at the 'difference' between the two quotes. Don't let him simply compare the two. So, for example, if you have a new conveyancing client who has been given a quote of £500 for the conveyancing on a move by another firm and your quote is £550, don't simply match it or go £20 below. Tell him this:

> "I can understand that you would want to get more than one quote *(People like people who understand them)*, but what we're really talking about here is £50, isn't it? *(ie, the difference between the two quotes)* Isn't it true, Mr Potter, that in order to complete the work, we could either do just enough to ensure a satisfactory conclusion or as much as possible to ensure that you have absolutely no worries. Now which would you prefer, just enough or as much as possible? Here we like to do as much as possible – would you think that's worth £50?"

- 'There's more work round the corner' – be wary of the client who asks for a cheap job on the basis that there is more work coming your way. There probably isn't. Normally, you should bill each job properly. Get each piece of work to pay its own way.

- Don't talk about the 'cost' of doing the work to the client. He thinks that cost is a word that's painful and nobody wants to know what it costs. Talk about the 'benefits' to that particular client.

> "I understand that you want to have your will completed by Friday and I guarantee that it can be done – and, I'll give you my home phone number in case you come across any problems while you're at home thinking about it. That way you'll have peace of mind."

- Talk about the 'investment' that the client is making.

> "The total investment to get your new business premises is £6,500".

If he thinks of it in terms of an investment it is far more positive and more likely to get a positive result.

- Remind the client that included in the fee is the reassurance that he will have **you** and your secretary at the end of the telephone.

- Give the client your home telephone number. Admittedly, this might sound shocking to a lot of lawyers. **Most clients will not phone you at home.** However, just the very fact of giving the phone number tells the client something about you – that you are considerate and realise that his situation is important, that you're both in there together trying to sort things out.

WHAT TO DO BEFORE YOU SEND THE BILL

If you have a bill that has been through your office procedure and, as far as your firm is concerned, it is a good and valid one, then you must consider whether to telephone the client before it is posted out. If it is for more than a few hundred pounds, the best advice is **always** to phone the client and tell her that you have prepared the bill, that it has been agreed with the billing partner and you are taking the courtesy of letting her know in advance the amount and that it will be coming out to her today.

That relieves the sting of the bill and gives you the chance to see what immediate reaction you get from your client. Remember, you want that client to be a life-time client and if she thinks that you are stinging her with an unacceptably high bill, then she won't be back again. However, if you explain why it is the size it is, then this will be appreciated.

You should also consider visiting your client to go through the bill if it is an especially high one.

None of this negates the requirement to give your client an idea about the size of the bill at the earliest possible stage. Also consider the desirability of getting the client to agree to monthly billing – this has a dramatic affect on your financial planning and your cash flow. Most business expenses are paid monthly, so if you can persuade clients to pay monthly, you will be better off and the client won't have a large cheque to write at the end of the work.

One cardinal rule to follow is that, once you have agreed a figure, you **must, must, must** stick to it. Even if the cost to you of doing the work has resulted in a loss for the firm, you must swallow that loss **no matter what.**

REMUNERATION CERTIFICATE

A client has an option to require the lawyer to obtain a remuneration certificate if he thinks the bill is too high. This is as a result of the *Solicitors' (Non-Contentious Business) Remuneration Order 1994 art 4(1)*. However, the right is lost if:

(a) the bill has been delivered and paid, or
(b) one month has elapsed after the lawyer has served a notice on the client containing the information about the client's entitlement to a remuneration certificate which complies with the Order, or
(c) the High Court orders a taxation or
(d) the lawyer and client have entered into a Non-Contentious Business Agreement.

If the lawyer has been frank with the client all along about billing and the cost of the work, then the bills should not be objectionable to the client. You want to keep your clients on the books and having them continually requesting remuneration certificates is not helpful.

GETTING AWAY FROM HOURLY BILLING

Most lawyers in England are still billing on an hourly basis. It will take many years for the system that has been developed over decades to change. However it is worth thinking about moving to a different type of billing. One that is becoming increasingly popular is the fixed fee. Here there is **no** need to have a **low** fee. But a fixed fee is beneficial to the clients who are, after all, the reason that the lawyer exists. As the American ideas about billing pervade this country's legal firms and more corporate clients insist on a different type of billing, then a variety of new methods will be found and employed by English firms.

THE NON-CONTENTIOUS BUSINESS AGREEMENT

In non-contentious matters, you can agree a fixed amount of costs with the client by way of a Non-Contentious Business Agreement. *(Section 57 Solicitors Act 1974)* These are good news but little used. Their use must be understood. There is no reason to think that you will be paid less than normal for this type of agreement. It fixes the amount that the lawyer can charge and has the advantage of being certain for both the lawyer and the client. It can be used at the start, during or at the end of some particular work. The best way is to get an agreement at the start of any particular piece of work. You should therefore have a clear idea as to what work needs to be undertaken on a particular job and know how much you will be charging and get the client's approval to that charge.

The agreement itself must show all the terms of the bargain, be in writing and signed by the person to be bound by the agreement or his agent. For goodness' sake, don't refer to it in front of the client as a 'Non-Contentious Business Agreement'. There is no need to bring in **our unique** language for the client! Call it a 'Representation Agreement' (ie, an agreement showing that you will be representing the client) or a 'Client Agreement'. Either of these is much less harsh and has the advantage that the client might actually understand what you're talking about.

The document can provide for the charge to be:

(a) a gross fixed sum

(b) a sum by reference to an hourly rate

(c) a sum by reference to a commission or percentage or 'otherwise' (there appear to be no definition of this term)

(d) a sum which shall include or shall not include all or any disbursements in respect of searches, plans, travelling, stamps, fees or other matters

The Section 57 agreement can be quite flexible. It is one that should be more widely used since it brings a level of some certainty about costs for the client and the lawyer. Certainly in so far as fixed cost are concerned, this is the type of agreement for the lawyer to use on a permanent basis. The agreement can be used to show at what intervals bills will be delivered. Lawyers pay a great many of their own bills on a monthly basis, so it is therefore sensible to get a monthly stream of money coming into the firm. Consequently, for appropriate cases, this type of agreement can be used to help the firm's cash flow.

This type of agreement also has the advantage to the lawyer that no remuneration certificate or taxing of the bill takes place. The agreement is a binding contract between the lawyer and the client.

Provided that you have complied with the conditions in Section 57, then the agreement will be a binding contract. However:

1   Section 57(5) provides that if a lawyer relies on it and the client objects to it as being unfair or unreasonable, a Taxing Officer may enquire into the facts and certify them to the court. If from the certificate it appears to the court that the agreement should be set aside, or the amount payable under it reduced, the court may so order. In addition the court may give other directions such as requiring an itemised bill to be prepared delivered and then taxed. 'From a practical point of view, the agreement of the client is the strongest evidence that the fee is reasonable.' *(Walton v Egan and others (1982) 3 All ER 849 Musthill J)*
If the agreement is enforced, then the matter may be referred to the Taxing Officer for inquiry and report, but on this reference, he acts as a delegate of the powers of the court and does not exercise his own originating powers of taxation.

2   Where the agreement refers to hourly rates, then on a taxation, if the client objects to the amount of the costs (but is not alleging

that the agreement is unfair or unreasonable) then the amount of the hourly rate will be binding on the client. However the Taxing Officer may enquire into (a) the number of hours worked and (b) whether the number of hours worked was excessive.

YET MORE STUFF TO CHECK OUT!

OFFICE MANUAL

An office manual is a loose-leaf book containing a wealth of information that readily gives a flavour of the firm. It is a vital insight into the firm for new staff. However, the manual should not be unalterable. It should be reviewed monthly and updated. These are not tablets of stone but methods of practice which have proved to be successful for the firm and ones which have helped to create the firm's culture.

This meticulously compiled manual should be the first book that the new person to the office sees on his or her first day. It should be carefully designed so that it looks appealing to read. The new staff member should spend a long time going through it with other members of the firm. The reasons why particular parts are included should be explained. The new person should be immersed in the firm's culture **before** starting his or her particular role. This process should include discussions with all levels of staff from senior partners to receptionists.

An Office Manual should contain the following:

* **Details of the structure of the firm**
  This should show names, hierarchies, responsibilities and team groupings, together with an organisation chart of the firm's structure. Detail **all** of the people who are in the office and their functions. Update this section immediately new staff are appointed.

(A useful extension of this idea has been successfully tried by many firms. A simplified structure chart, with photographs of the principal players is displayed in the foyer or reception area. This allows newcomers and visitors to put faces to names and presents a clear view of the organisation and its major elements.)

- **A mission statement for the firm**
  Copies of this can also be printed and given to clients, as well as being displayed in the reception area, for example.

- **A section on the importance of the client to the firm**
  This should outline the firm's underlying philosophy.

- **A style section**
  This comprehensive section should detail everything that needs to be known about the way the firm puts across its differentiated message – it should cover everything from the layout of letters to the layout of the office itself.

- **A statement about best judgment**
  This is a clear statement that the firm's people are empowered to take action on behalf of the firm and that their best judgment should be used at all times.

It is however important to remember that the Law Society does have special Rules to ensure that legal advice is not dispensed by unqualified staff. But quite often, any situation can be resolved by the present members of the firm using their 'best judgment'.

A Federal Express employee in America used his best judgment one night. The Company arranges the passage of parcels around America with the slogan 'Absolutely, Positively Overnight'. They guarantee that a parcel posted one day will arrive by 10am the following morning. The Company's customers do not want to hear that, because of a truck breakdown in some part of the country, their vital package had not got through. They want to hear the guarantee and see it being backed up every night by **action** from the Company that shows them keeping to that amazing promise as reiterated by their slogan.

One night, there was a major headache for a particular local manager. He could see that parcels were not going to get through unless he did something drastic. He did something quite extraordinary – he hired a helicopter and paid for it on his own credit card to ensure that the Company's guarantee was met and they kept to their side of the contract.

Encourage your people to use their best judgment to sort out problems and not simply pass the buck or sit on them.

- **A list of words which are banned**

  Experience will tell you which words are often misunderstood by clients – and even by lawyers and their staffs. Many words are contentious and misleading, or have specific (often legal) meanings that clients might misunderstand. Assemble a list of these difficult words and phrases by canvassing your teams and publish the results. This should be clear and explanatory. Examples might include:

  - *'obviously'* – we just love it, don't we! The trouble is, it may be obvious to us but usually it isn't to the client

  - *'in this matter'* – it is not a 'matter' to the client – it is a lot more important than that.

  - *'the child Phillip'* – for some reason, this type of phrase peppers matrimonial files – the first two words are unnecessary and referring to Phillip as a person is much less harsh.

- **Stylistic conventions for written material and letters**

  Insist on the following:

- never use a long word where a short one will do
- do not be sarcastic
- do not be stuffy or pompous
- use simple sentences
- keep paragraphs short
- avoid indecisive words.

- **Confidentiality**

  An important section in the manual must deal with the business of confidentiality. Clients do not want their private matters to be known around the town. It is therefore **vital** that **all** your people must know that they are not allowed to talk about clients' matters outside the office. Nor must they even confirm or deny that a particular person is a client of the firm. The Law Society has very strict rules on confidentiality and it is up to you to ensure that all your people know about them.

  Also make it a practice not to tell your spouse or partner what is going on in the office so far as the clients are concerned. You will find that if you do, then secrets leak out. If a spouse or partner knows nothing, then there is no possibility of a breach.

- **Competitors**

  Recognise that the firm has competitors and detail them in the manual. Show the new employee which local banks have Executor and Trustee Services, who are the licensed conveyancers, the will making firms and the other firms of solicitors in the town. Remember that the other firms are in competition with you. The client has a choice. He will see the other firms as competition and you have to ensure that the client comes to you and then stays with you.

  Include in the manual a caution that your lawyers do not discuss the competition with clients – there is no need to mention them. It simply gives them a recognition that you do not need to give them. Do not compare your firm with any other firm in the presence of clients. It is not professional and just shows your clients that you are prepared to bad-mouth the competition.

- **You do not do that sort of work**
  The manual should include a procedure for dealing with work that the firm does not normally handle.

  You may find that one of your clients needs legal advice of a kind that your firm does not have. Tell the client that your firm have no specialists for the kind of advice required. Explain that you can recommend another lawyer and then phone the other lawyer to arrange the first meeting. If you can take your client to the other lawyer and introduce them, so much the better. The second lawyer should recognise that he is being trusted to do this one job but that the client belongs to you. If he tries to poach your client, then cut him off your list of recommended lawyers.

- **List of Counsel**
  Develop a list of the Counsel you use and the subjects they specialise in. Update the list regularly and refer to the list in the manual.

- **Library of Opinions**
  As you receive Opinions from barristers, keep a separate copy in a library for future reference. They can become a valuable resource of the firm. Refer to this library in the manual.

- **Banking**
  Detail the Banking procedure you have and the 'Stop Cheque System' you operate (see page 116).

- **Procedures**
  Detail the procedure you adopt for file management and any other procedures which your firm have developed.

- **Referrals**
  Include in this section the details of the people that your firm refer work and clients to. Include the Banks, Building Societies, professional contacts, lawyers and any other contacts you have.

Regularise this aspect of your business and monitor what referrals you make.

- **New Business Co-ordinator**

  Detail the role of the new business co-ordinator and his or her function in the office. Ensure that your people know who it is and what is the function of the co-ordinator. Ensure that they gladly accept calls from this person with new clients who have been seen and are ready to pass on to other firm members.

- **Marketing**

  Here you can place information about your marketing activities. If you have a marketing department, then give details here. If you have advertisements in papers, magazines or wherever, put a copy in the manual so that your people will know what the firm is saying. Any current campaigns must also be detailed here together with an acknowledgement that marketing is the function of everybody in the office.

- **Financial Services**

  Give details of the services you provide under the financial services heading. This is an excellent service to provide and compliments so many departments in the office. It is hard to justify **not** having such a service.

- **Client Conflict**

  Describe the procedure you go through to ensure that there is no conflict with an existing client when taking on a new client.

The prime purpose of the office manual is to provide a wealth of practical information about the workings of the firm. It must be kept totally up to date and must be readily available to anyone who may need to refer to it. Too often an apology for an office manual is kept stuffed in some distant cupboard and when located, is found to be last updated several years before. That clearly is inefficient and pointless.

If the manual is carefully constructed, then a photocopy can be made up for each new employee. But bear in mind that each copy will also need to be updated regularly along with the master copy. Better still is to have the office manual on your computer so that every change can be made instantly and a simple print-run organised at will.

THE NEWSLETTER

Keeping in touch with the client is vital, and you should be forever thinking of ways to do so. A newsletter is an excellent way of doing so on a regular basis. **But**, you need to follow some rules:

- Once you have decided on, say, a three-monthly publication, make sure you send one every three months. Do not let it lapse.

- Get the thing properly designed by a graphic designer. Do not design it yourself.

- Make sure that the newsletter is readable and has short items about a variety of topics.

- Include sections about non-legal items, and you will reinforce the idea that you have a wider interest for your clients.

THE RECEPTIONIST'S MANUAL

The people you have in the offices must be told that the receptionist/telephonist's room is the **most important** one in the whole building. The first point of contact with the firm for all clients is the receptionist/telephonist. Her task (and it usually is a female who covers this aspect of the firm's work) is absolutely vital.

She **must** be fully trained to deal with whatever comes her way. She must know the philosophy of the firm and your mission statement. She must know who does what, who the new business co-ordinator is, what the firm's policy is on callers-in to the office, and how the telephone should be answered.

So prepare a special manual just for her. She will then realise that you regard her office as absolutely vital. On appointment, she should have **at least a week** learning all about the firm and seeing precisely how it is run and how the firm expects her to run her office. She should know the office manual backwards.

Get her on a telephone answering course, an 'excellence sells' course, a listening course, a marketing course. Persuade her to go on a thirteen week Dale Carnegie Human Relations course. Empower her to take decisions and responsibility. She is pivotal – your investment in her will show to her that she is taken and accepted as an important member of the firm.

She can listen to the clients and pick up information that she can pass on to you. It may be something to do with a financial investment – the client's mother has just inherited some money and is looking for an investment, the client works for a manufacturing company and the boss hasn't prepared any contracts of employment – get in there and sell your services. She can **always** be on the look-out for extra work. Your investment will pay off. You will be amazed at how your investment in her will reap rewards often in ways that you can never foresee.

An additional duty these days, sad to report, is to deal with sudden emergencies, particularly in areas which may be racially or politically sensitive. Devise a clear set of instructions that must be followed if alarms sound, threatening calls are received or persons of dubious character invade the premises.

Timewasters and cranks also have a sneaky habit of entering warm office premises with the intent of dallying out of the cold and wasting valuable time in pointless conversation with the inhabitants. At the top end of the scale, advise your receptionists what to do if there should be physical threats of violence or, even worse, a bomb scare.

Once you have recruited a good receptionist, don't forget to include her in your training programmes. You should include her in in-house on-going training as well as one-off courses. Train, train, train! Reward her for her enthusiasm and commitment. Recognise her achievements and contribution to the firm. Get your bonus/incentive system geared up to include **all** members of your office team.

CLIENT REGISTRATION FORM

When you see clients for the first time, you need to get as much information about them as possible. Have a simple form or card prepared that is:

(a) a reminder to the lawyer to complete the information gathering

(b) so designed that seeking and recording the information is easy.

You can then enter these details into your computer so that cross-selling can take place at a later date, birthday cards can be sent and financial services and product details are sent to the appropriate clients. You cannot know your clients and their families too well. Acquire their home, business and mobile phone numbers. Tell your clients that they are now a registered clients with the firm and that entitles them to a free financial service check-up or whatever. **Super-please your clients.**

THE 'THANK YOU' FILE

Everybody in the office should have one of these. Possibly two of the most important words in the English language are 'Thank you'. When they are said with feeling, they are a powerful statement. When, as a lawyer, you say it to a client or indeed anybody, then they have a special significance that most lawyers do not appreciate. We have already looked at the importance of thanking people who recommend work to you. There are others who should be included in this important, personal file:

• If someone sees you in the street and passes on some information, write a short thank-you note.

• If you get taken to lunch or for a drink, write to that person to offer your personal thanks.

- Any time someone does something for you, no matter how small, then drop them a thank-you note.

FILE MANAGEMENT

It is **vital** that the files you have are in good order. It makes finding things much easier. So, for example, it is common practice to keep the correspondence separate from the documents that are produced.

A simple index sheet at the front of the file helps enormously.

As you become more client orientated, you need to have information at the front of the file about the client. For example, all relevant phone numbers should be prominent together with times when the client likes to be phoned. If you have a business client who always has his office meetings in the mornings between 9 and 11am, then make a note of this on the file so that you do not phone him during those hours and interrupt his meeting. Ask your clients at their initial interview whether there are good and bad times to contact them. This will show that you care. You will super-please your client.

Get into the frame of mind to do as much as possible for the client.

There is a hotel I read about recently where one guest returned for his second visit. He was first of all greeted by name at the reception desk and was told. "Mr Smith, you said last time you were here that you liked the view from your bedroom window so I've arranged for the same room that you stayed in last time to be available for you." Mr Smith was very impressed. Not only had they taken note of what he said on his last visit but they had acted on it this time.

If you have a client who expresses a particular like or dislike, then act upon it whenever you can. Make a note of it in front of the file and it is there to refer to every time the file is opened.

Find out if the client prefers a weekly or monthly report, black coffee, two copies of each document – whatever – find out and note it and act upon it. This is a marvellous opportunity for you to individualise your service for each client – something that the business world has been trying to do for years.

THE BUSINESS CARD

There is one major problem with **all** lawyers' business cards – they are not used enough!

Business cards should be well printed and designed and then handed out as much as possible. They are a great advert for your firm. They should be given to friends, family, clients, contacts, anyone you meet on the train who talks about legal work, everyone who recommends work to you, anyone who asks about the firm.

You should not have the pile of a hundred cards that you received two years ago from the printers going mouldy in your bottom drawer. You **must** carry them with you wherever you go. If you hand out cards to anyone who expresses an interest, you will be amazed to find who rings you with work. But they won't do so if you have to write your name and address on the back of an envelope. That is not professional and you must be professional at all times. So keep business cards on you, at home, in the office, in the car – everywhere you can think of.

Have something unusual on the card. How about 'PROBLEM BUSTER'?

If you are in the financial services field (and most lawyers should be), then put on your card 'I BUY INSURANCE'. When the potential client asks you what this means, you can say, "I buy insurance at the lowest possible cost and for the maximum possible benefit for my clients – would you like me to buy some for **you**?"

Also think about putting the name of your spouse or partner on the card. It will make your clients feel more comfortable if they have to ring you at home. They then know the name of your partner and so can talk to him or her as a person. Do not forget that you are trying to build a relationship with your clients that will last a lifetime. Any small indications from you that you are **human** goes a long way with clients. They probably won't phone you at home but the fact that you are thinking about your clients has been shown on the card that the client keeps. It's psychological but it **works!**

For special occasions, it is possible to produce quite acceptable business cards on the computer. Several companies produce specially cut A4 sheets which allow you to make up to 16 cards at a time, with smooth edges just like the printer's cards.

With the advice of your graphic designer, have some cards made that emphasise a particular offer, an event that your company is involved in sponsoring or whatever. These cards can be adjusted very easily on the computer to accommodate the names and titles of different members of the firm.

Other versions of these cards can be given out at local events such as school fetes or sports matches. A card is more easily tucked away for future reference than a more bulky brochure. There is business out there.

WHAT BUSINESS ARE YOU IN?

Whilst having dinner in a restaurant one day, the Chairman of Rolex, Andre Heininger, was stopped by a friend who asked, "How's the watch business?" Heininger replied, "I have no idea." His friend laughed. Here was the head of the world's most prestigious watchmakers saying that he didn't know what was going on in his own industry. But Heininger was deadly serious. "Rolex is not in the watch business – we are in the luxury business." An interesting story.

I wonder what your reply would be to the question, "How's the legal business?" Would you say, "The conveyancing world is a pain", or "The matrimonial work is slowing down."

Really you are in the **people business**. Remember what we all forget. Without the client you would have no work. The **client super-pleasing business** is what you're in.

TRAINING

The training of staff must never be underestimated.

For legal staff, it is essential that they are up to date with the latest legislation and developments in their chosen branches of the profession. They should therefore go on every up-dating course they can for their speciality as well as reading the current 'professional' literature that will give them a sound oversight of what is new and important.

All your staff – legal and non-legal – should have tuition in marketing their services. All the office staff are involved in marketing and they should all be aware of it and be proficient in it. In-house and outside courses should be chosen.

In addition, the Dale Carnegie Human Relations course is an essential for your people. It is a 13-week evening course that will help them tremendously.

Of your other office staff, the receptionist is one to single out for top treatment. A telephone answering techniques course has to be a must for all your reception staff.

Your people are your most expensive and important investments. If you treat them all as lifetime employees and expect the best from them, a funny thing happens – you often get the best.

Your people must be recognised as the important people that they are. You can do this in the following ways:

• **Staff Titles**
  Traditionally, solicitors' offices had the following job descriptions:

  • Consultant
  • Partner
  • Assistant Solicitor
  • Cashier
  • Secretary
  • Receptionist

It is now time to create some new job descriptions that reward your staff. How about:

- Associate Solicitor
- Director of Finance
- Personal Assistant
- Client Services Associate.

Rewarding your team with distinctive client function titles pleases them.

- **Bonuses and financial rewards**
  In order to benefit your people, some form of recognition of their services to the client needs to be put in place. There are partnerships that divide the net profits to the partners on the basis of the number and extent of super-pleased clients. The clients are surveyed to find out how they regard their legal representatives, who are then paid accordingly. For non-legal members of staff, this can be done too. Also consider the benefit of marketing to the established client. It is much cheaper to market new services to an existing client than to a new one. So, instead of leaning all the benefits towards the rainmaker who gets new clients, distribute some benefits to the staff who are cross-selling to existing clients.

- **Meetings**
  Recognise that your people have a good deal to contribute to the firm. They have ideas that you may not even have dreamed of. Gather them together and brainstorm some ideas from them and reward any good ones that come out of the session.

- **Certificates**
  Most people are delighted to receive certificates. Have some specially designed and printed for your firm. Celebrate the winners of these certificates and make them cherished possessions. Reward the best staff member of the month, the one who has done the most for a client that month, the best story about

helping a client. But above all, make sure that they are sincerely given.

- **Retreats**

  Getting away from the office environment for a while can do wonders for the staff. Organise a retreat to another part of the country where you can do some brainstorming, present some certificates, tell the staff what is coming up in the next year and have some quality time together – which must include some social entertainment. Make it a memorable event by doing something unusual.

  If you have some serious training to do, then it is a sound policy to do it out of the office if at all possible. Try a local hotel or borrow someone else's training resource. This gives the staff the opportunity to concentrate on the new learning without the constant irritation of telephone calls, interruptions and other distractions that inevitably occur when training is conducted on your own premises. Learning is improved and the training is given greater credibility by being seen as a high priority.

- **Pay**

  Staff do work for pay. Try to be one of the best payers around. But expect the best from your people.

ADOPT THE CONCEPT THAT IN ORDER TO ACHIEVE UNUSUAL RESULTS, SOMETIMES IT IS NECESSARY TO TAKE UNUSUAL ACTIONS

Don't run with the crowd.

- Be the first to introduce a new service in your area.

- Redesign your stationery.

- Sponsor your local amateur football team.

- Offer a prize for local schoolchildren in an essay writing competition – choose a topic that has some association with the legal profession.

- Enter a float in the local carnival.

- Advertise a special discount day for some specific services and have an open day for new clients

Would you be brave enough to adopt Osborne Clarke's orange prowling cat on your letter heading? Light the front of your office in blue or green – something that shows that you stand out from the crowd. Let the world see that you are around and that you care.

MOMENTS OF TRUTH

Jan Carlzon became the President of Scandinavian Airlines (SAS) in the 1980s. The company at that time was doing appallingly. He realised that their customers' perception of the company was formed at the times when his staff and the customers came into contact. He carried out a survey and found that each of his customers came into contact with five of the SAS employees on each transaction. Each of these meetings he termed a 'moment of truth' – a moment when the company had to prove to its customers that they were the best option from all the possibilities in the market place. They had therefore to manage those moments of truth to shine in the eyes of their customers and start attracting customer loyalty. This he did impressively well.

He realised that **information** was the key to getting his staff to be able to react to customer queries and requests. He believed that an individual without information cannot take responsibility whereas an individual with information could not help but take responsibility. His training was therefore geared up to ensuring that his staff knew what was going on, what the menu on the plane was, how long the flight would take, what kind of vegetarian food was available, how wheelchairs were dealt with and so on. Using this technique, his staff never had to say, "I don't know." They were there with the answer to the customers' requests at every moment of truth. He managed these moments to perfection. It meant that his front-line employees were trained and empowered to deal with whatever came their way. This made all the difference in the perception of the Airline that the customers had formed.

Remember that every time a client contacts your office, a **moment of truth** is created, whether it is with you, your receptionist, cashier, assistant secretary, partner, PA, trainee lawyer, legal executive, the tea lady or whoever works with you. It is their reaction to the client that is important. It reflects the office philosophy. It has to be managed and staff must be given the authority to deal with the problems and queries that the clients have. They must take responsibility – take control. They must not be forever passing the buck to someone else. Or saying that they just don't know because you've never told them. Get them involved in the client process, the decisions that affect the clients. Bring them into the meetings. Get staff that are **passionate** to serve your firm's clients and not just prepared tolerate them.

As a spin-off benefit of training, employees take responsibility for their work. They come to develop the passion which is present in the owners of the business – a desire to be as helpful as possible and to do as much as possible and not just enough to get by.

There is a wonderful story about two stone masons chipping away at square blocks of granite in a quarry. One was asked what he was doing. He replied that he was "cutting this damn stone into a block." The other said, "I'm on this team that's building a cathedral." They were both doing the same job but their attitudes were entirely different. Get your team building a cathedral.

WORD OF MOUTH MARKETING

Picture the scene. It is coffee time. Some neighbours have got together and now have a regular weekly meeting while their children play around on the floor or in the next room. Coffee and biscuits are on the menu and a good chat is the outcome. All sorts of topics are raised. One day, because one of them is thinking of moving house, the discussion turns to the choice of lawyer to pick for the conveyancing work. One of the mothers says, *"Well, I think that Jones and Partners are awful. It takes them ages to reply to letters and they never get their accounts right."*

That statement is enough to stop all the people there from going anywhere near Jones and Partners for any legal work at all. This shows the power of word of mouth.

Moving this to the business world, word of mouth is probably the most powerful form of communication in the business environment. We know what it is like to get recommendations from colleagues, to go to the training conference rather than simply read the notes. The interaction there is terribly important. We pick up pointers – what others feel about their professionals, how things are. It is all word of mouth and yet it affects our decisions and often in very basic ways. Your choice of which barrister to instruct, which computer to buy, which estate agent to sell the firm's building – all these decisions can be affected by word of mouth recommendation. It was the only form of marketing allowed by the Law Society until the 1980s and a lot of our senior brethren remember only ever getting work as a result of recommendations or word of mouth.

It is so important and yet most of us do nothing to affect the possible outcome of such recommendations.

How can this be changed?

First of all we must accept that much word of mouth is out of control of the firm. But not all! To this end, a word of mouth campaign will help.

Advantages of a word of mouth campaign

*   **Individual message**
    The message that you are trying to get across can be tuned to the individual listener. It can therefore be flexible and be altered to suit the recipient.

*   **Instant feedback**
    You know instantly what effect your campaign is having because of the instant feedback you will get. You can then adjust the message as necessary.

*   **An experienced process**
    The marketing here is actually experienced by the listener. It is marketing where he hears the words, listens to the tone of voice, sees the non-verbal signs of the talker. It is therefore an experiencing process for the listener. It is an experience that

thousands of business people enjoy and it is the reason that they travel often thousands of miles to hear and see, rather than merely read about. Remember the conferences you have been to and the better message that you came away with as a result of actually being there and experiencing the talk. It does mean that passion can come over in the message as well.

As a word of warning, it must be remembered that word of mouth of a negative type is just as powerful, as in the case of the coffee morning example. Letting bad vibes circulate about your firm can be devastating and any source of such bad-mouthing must be stopped if at all possible. Think of some recent company shareholders' meetings where a vociferous group manages to sway the rest, and the media, with their accusatory rhetoric.

• Then there is the 90-10 Rule which states that 90% of the world is influenced by the other 10%. So if you can reach that 10%, they will in turn help you by influencing the other 90%.

How to do it:

ONE   First of all, you must decide what message you are trying to put across.

TWO   Then decide who should receive the message.

THREE   Finally, you need to sort out who in your firm should deliver the message.

Suppose, for example, you decide to target the 20-30 female age range to take advantage of your Financial Services check-up and will making services. First, acquire a list of those clients you already have who are in that category. Have a meeting in the office and see which of those are the 10%ers. In other words, which of those females have quite dominant personalities and may be able to influence others. Your people in the office will know their clients and should be able to tell you precisely who fits the bill. Decide where else this target group might assemble – with which wider groups might they associate. Work out precisely what **benefit** these individuals will have by taking advantage of your services or the message you want to put over and how you are going to contact them. Remember, there must be a benefit to them. People buy services because of the benefit or result to them.

Other sources of good word of mouth advertising

There are a number of ways of encouraging people to speak about you and your firm in a favourable fashion. These ideas may involve you in a little bit of research, some writing and ordering and a dose of energy but the possible outcomes can be most beneficial.

* Produce a small booklet, even as small as one-eighth of A4, which contains a list of useful service providers in your area or town. These can be people that you have dealt with from your firm, clients in business or just people who have been recommended to you. Of course, your firm's name will appear prominently on the covers. Give these away freely. People will talk about it and maybe the other service providers listed will recommend their customers and clients to you.

* Whenever you send out an information leaflet, a brochure or one of the above little booklets, send out two. Suggest in any covering letter that your client should pass the second copy on to a friend or acquaintance. That way, your firm will get talked about even more widely.

* Produce a simple postcard that you can send in your ordinary mail to clients, which suggests that they should send it on to someone else who might be pleased to hear of your services. The text of the card might read something like:

I have just received some excellent advice from ABC Solicitors. They also sent me some useful leaflets that you never seem to get from other solicitors. They have asked me to send this card to a friend, relative or associate who might also benefit from a legal service that offers something different. I thought of you. They tell me that there is no obligation, no follow-up, no passing on of your name and address and no pressure. They just want to let people know about their services. Post back this card in an envelope. They said that they would then send you their current brochure to let you see what services they offer. This sounds reasonable to me.

Signed _____

Such a simple idea, at very little cost, can increase your potential client list very easily. People will talk about it.

• Somewhat more elaborate but still a good talking point would be a simple website with information of general interest about your services and the law. If you have a particular specialism, mention that too. People will talk about it.

UNDER-PROMISE – OVER-DELIVER

In which of the following situations would you think that you had given the better service?

1   On Monday morning, a commercial client instructs you to prepare a draft lease of a 30-unit shopping complex. You tell him that it will be available in three days – on Wednesday at 10am. In fact, you deliver it to him the day after, on Thursday morning at 10am. You had some difficulty in getting the final draft agreed by one of the Partners.

2   Same lease, same instructions. But here you tell the client
that it will be available on Friday at 10am. In fact, you get it to
him on Thursday morning at 10am.

In the second situation, the client is pleased because he received the
lease one day earlier than you said, even though in real terms you
delivered the thing a day later than in the first situation. In the second
situation, you have a happy client. In the first situation, you have an
unhappy one who now cannot believe what you say about delivery of
documents. So the simple message is – under-promise, then over-
deliver, thereby super-pleasing the client.

FINANCIAL SERVICES

If you currently do not have a section in your office that deals with
financial services, then you really ought to think carefully about
having one. It is a wonderful method of getting new work for the firm.
As the client's trusted adviser, why shouldn't you be providing this
service to the client? Why let it be a tied agent from a single insurance
body who cannot give truly independent advice to your client. There
are so many different financial products that your clients need and
want as they progress through the years and so many spin-offs. There
are few departments in the office who cannot recommend that their
clients see the financial services experts in your office, so the
opportunities for cross-selling are enormous.

There is a major headache for lawyers because they are governed
by their Professional Rules and in particular, the one that relates to the
way commissions on such products are dealt with. The *Solicitors'
Practice Rules 1990* state that a Solicitor must account to his client for
any commission received of more than £20 unless, having disclosed
the amount of the commission, or the basis of calculation if the
amount cannot be be ascertained, he has the client's agreement to
retain it.

Now this would seem on the face of it to put a damper on the
selling of financial services products which are rewarded by the
payment of commissions by the insurance companies. If the whole of
the commission has to go to the client, what is the point of selling

them the product and deriving no benefit for the lawyer? The answer is to turn this disadvantage to your benefit. Tell your client that if he uses your services, commissions of £x will be paid by the insurance company and that that money belongs to him. Tell him that if he wishes to use your independent advice, then your firm's policy is to split the commission under whatever arrangement you have – and would he be willing to proceed on that basis? You may decide to let him have all the commission and simply charge him for the advice. Whatever you decide to do, have the client sign an authority form agreeing to the arrangement.

REMEMBER THE CHILDREN

If a client comes into the office with children, then you must be prepared for this. Your receptionist must know what to do to welcome them. Purchase a jar of sweets to have on hand for the children and instruct the receptionist to ask the parent if she can hand some to the child.

See what else you can do in the reception area for those occasions when a child comes in. Most parents are anxious about bringing children into an office, so it is up to you to calm these fears and make their visit as welcome as possible.

Also consider what happens to the child if he or she comes with the parent into your room. The parents want to hear what you have to say, so have some sensible diversions ready for the children. If you have a side desk, produce some paper and crayons or pencils and see if you can persuade the child to sit and draw.

The parents will be delighted that you have taken this trouble and the child will remember that the place is not such a bad place to visit after all. It may even encourage them to come to you when they are old enough to need legal advice. Super-please the client.

RHINOS

RHINOS are people in the firm who are

> **R**eally
> **H**ere
> **I**n
> **N**ame
> **O**nly

You don't want these people in your firm. If your vetting procedure is good enough, then you should have spotted these people a mile off. However if you have **any people at all** in the firm who really are not interested in the place; who regard clients as a pain and make no contribution to the office; who think that this business would be all right if it wasn't for the clients; then **get rid of them! Fast!**

You cannot afford these days to have people who are Really Here In Name Only. They have a terribly dispiriting effect on the rest of your people and that effect will spread like a cancer among the remaining members of the firm unless it is rooted out quickly. So **no matter who it is**, and even if you if you have to pay redundancy pay, remove the rhino as soon as you can.

The remaining members of staff will have seen what has been going on and will not believe in your philosophy unless you take this positive, pruning action. You have got to have the courage of your convictions, as clearly stated in your mission statement and philosophy.

Such an exercise will often have a sharpening effect on the rest of the staff who will recognise that the skivers they have been carrying for some time have at last received their just desserts.

ORPHANS

An orphan is someone who appears in your neighbourhood, who needs looking after. For example, if you read in the local newspaper about a new assistant bank manager coming to town, then contact him or her immediately. Do it before anybody else does.

Take the newcomer to lunch. Present the firm's information pack. Explain the firm's philosophy and make this person feel welcome. After the lunch, write to thank her for coming out with you. Maintain regular contact by letter and phone. She will remember your firm as the first point of contact she had in town.

When she is trying to think who to recommend, there is a good chance that your firm's name will be at the front of her mind.

Add this new professional colleague to your party list, your Christmas card list, your birthday card list.

MAKE FRIENDS WITH CLIENTS AND CONTACTS

Remember this?

**PEOPLE LIKE PEOPLE
WHO ARE LIKE THEY ARE**

If your client thinks '... well, this lawyer is a little bit like me', then you have a chance of establishing a good rapport with that client. The way you do that is:

- agree with his opinions

- if you cannot agree with his opinion because, as his lawyer, you know that what he is saying is wrong, then you can **always** agree with the thought process behind the opinion. Say to the client, *"I can understand how you feel that"*, or *"I can understand why you think that"*.

He will then be much more inclined to accept what you say because you are now a little bit like him. You understand why he holds a

111

particular view. He can then feel that his lawyer is on the same wavelength and will be able to understand his problems and help him sort them out.

One of the easiest ways of showing an interest in the client is to ask questions and **listen** to what the client tells you (remember the 'third ear' concept). So, to help super-please the client:

- become genuinely interested in what he tells you
- use the client's name often in the conversation
- be a good listener
- talk in terms of the other person's interests
- try to use some of the same words that the client uses
- make the client feel important
- get on first name terms with the client as soon as you can.

A MISSION STATEMENT

Prepare for yourself a mission or policy statement. It will help to bind the firm together. It will show to your people what you care about and your focus. Avoid statements that simply say that you will 'provide a quality service to clients'. That is what all lawyers want to do. Think up one that is special to **your firm** alone. Have a look at the mission statements of the large companies of the world. See if they give you any inspiration.

Set your sights high and give yourself a solid target to aim at – your mission statement must resonate with enthusiasm and promise for a better future, both for yourselves and your clients.

Once you have written one, then live it!

- **Include it on your literature.**
- **Show it in reception.**
- **Remind your people of it by having it displayed in the offices.**
- **Live it and love it.**

MOVE INTO THE INFORMATION BUSINESS

When we looked at super-pleasing the client by sending quality, beneficial printed material, we saw that by sending your client copies of an extract of an Act that dealt with her particular problem and producing a bill that was sensible, the client was more inclined to pay more for the service. That is because you were adding value to the advice you were giving. Because the advice on its own is intangible, you need to make it tangible by giving your client additional information in a format that can be handled. For example, if you are sending a draft will for the client to approve, then send with it a printed brochure or form or information sheet that is professional and can provide additional information about the will. Give your client information – add value to your service by giving her more than she expected.

There is a great deal of mystique about the legal profession and the convoluted legal ways of solicitors, so the more you can unravel the mysteries and set ideas and practices down in good, plain English for your clients, the better will be their acceptance of your services. Think about having a simple series of attractive, explanatory leaflets which can be handed out to clients or enquirers, which cover your main activities.

Super-please your client.

HOW TO GET MORE LEGAL WORK FROM EXISTING CLIENTS

* **Super-duper-please your special clients**
  A super-pleased client is worth her weight in gold. She is your best source of new business. If she is delighted with you then she will quite happily recommend you to her friends. Ask for recommendations. Remember to write and thank her for any recommendation. Also phone her on occasions. If you have a new service that you think she would be interested in, then phone her and tell her about it. Ask her if she can give you the names of any

friends who might be interested as well. **Ask for the business**. Remember that to produce unusual results, sometimes you have to use unusual methods and for lawyers, just asking for the business is unusual.

The problem about seeking recommendations is that, although a client may be happy with your service, she will not recommend you unless the topic of lawyers comes up. Should the topic of you or your firm arise, then she would be delighted to recommend you. So you need to get the subject mentioned more often. You can do that by anchoring the client's pleasure by tying it into a symbol that the client often uses. A special pen, a personalised Filofax or some other article that you believe the client will have with her constantly. Then your valued client will have a constant reminder of you and your firm. She is then more likely to recommend you. Clearly, you cannot do this for every client and you will have to decide who to chose as appropriate recipients.

Follow these rules:

- Make the gift unique or ensure it has a scarcity factor – some novelty that will make it unique or special to her so that she will be reminded of you whenever she sees it.

- Make the gift have a greater significance for the client. Give her a certificate specially produced that acknowledges her importance or contribution to the firm. Get the certificate specially designed and produced to look professional. Then present it to her.

- Personalise the gift as much as you can.

- If you have an especially good client, then do something to recognise that she is important. Take her to the theatre, golfing, an exhibition or wherever the client would like to go. Reinforce the occasion with a photograph taken at the time.

Get it specially framed. Buy a book of the film/show/musical and put an endorsement in it.

- **Use your Diary**

  Enter future events in your diary, that you know will affect your client and write to her beforehand to remind her of the events. Anything can be included here. Court dates, licensing renewals and lease renewals, will update periods, new legislation etc.

- **Rental periods**

  Write to your clients at least three months before any new rental period. Tell them about your services to negotiate on their behalf.

- **Wills**

  Every four years, contact every client for whom you have made a will to ask them to ensure that their wills are up to date or whether any changes need to be made. Tie in a suggestion about a financial services free review.

- **Clients about to reach 18 years of age**

  If you have a trust which has children under 18 years who are due shortly to reach their majority, then write to them. Tell them what the procedure is for them to have access to any inheritance monies. Schedule an appointment for them to come and see your financial services people totally free of charge and without obligation, to go through the advantages of looking after their monies properly.

- **Newspapers, Law Reports and Statutes**

  When you are scanning through these various papers, if you find anything of interest to a client, then copy it and sent it to him. Don't bill him for it but send a note saying that you thought he might be interested in the copy. If he wants to get any further information tell him he can contact you.

- **Newsletters**
  Make sure you send a newsletter to every client.

- **Firm's Client Registration Card**
  If you use client registration cards, then check them regularly to see if there is anything there that would help you cross-sell any of your services to a client. Remember in particular your will making services and your financial services department or contact.

THE 'STOP CHEQUE' SYSTEM

Before any client receives money from the firm, you must arrange to speak to him about what he is going to do with it. This is not just poking your nose in when it is not wanted. It is good practice and excellent advice. For example, a client who receives a £50,000 cheque as a result of an inheritance may well decide – without telling you – that he is going to invest some of it. You should be ready to suggest the services of your financial services section or contact so that the client benefits from some independent advice. He may be lead away by a tied agent who can only suggest his company's products.

Give the client the opportunity to use your services. Remember that he is entitled to keep all the commission, which is another bonus in using the services of his lawyer. You will benefit by getting the agreement of the client to any commission splitting or fee-based arrangement that you and the client negotiate for your service. You will then have done the client some good and increased the profits of your firm.

Use this arrangement when a client is expecting:

- the sale proceeds of a property
- monies from the administration of an estate
- an insurance settlement
- a dispute settlement
- or whenever you have money that belongs to the client.

LOOK FOR MONEY

You should be on the look out for money all the time. Listen to what clients say about money, investments, insurance. Ask your clients if they have any monies to invest and would they like an obligation-free chat with your financial services person. Tell them that they do not need to have millions to invest and tell them about the commission policy of your firm.

Ask your clients if they are happy with the rate of interest that they are receiving – tell them that you will search for another source and that for other clients in the past, you have managed to increase their interest return. Do **not** say that you definitely will be able to get a better return because you know nothing at that stage about the clients' finances. Tell them that you have been successful in the past and can prepare a free confidential no-obligation report.

DRESS THE PART

In order to be a professional, you need to look the part. Dress in a professional manner. Bear in mind the different types of legal service providers we were discussing a few pages back – the corporate client lawyer and the burglars' lawyer. Clearly you will need to dress appropriately for your client group to feel comfortable in your presence. This should not mean being wildly eccentric, because you will still need to maintain your professionalism and keep up your personal standards.

THE MONTHLY FILE CHECK

You should be actively working on a good percentage of the files in your cabinet. There are some however that, for one reason or another, have little or no work that needs to be done on them for long periods of time. Adopt a strategy to check **all** the files once a month to make sure you haven't missed anything important. I appreciate that many offices have computer memory jogs or diary notes and these are extremely useful. However you should back this up by going through the filing cabinet to check that nothing is missed. Do it when you won't be interrupted.

Once you have honed the cabinet down to really active files, you should be able to get through the cabinet quickly. You will also feel a sense of well-being that comes from knowing that you are on top of everything that you are working on.

THE LARGE PILE OF FILES THAT ALL NEED ATTENTION

If you go through the cabinet and pull out masses of files that all need some attention, then before you do anything on them, sort them out into various piles. Do the easy files **first.** That will then decrease the total workload and give you an early sense of achievement that something substantial has been done. Then, methodically work through the other files. Do not do it all at once. Do it over a few days. When it is time for the next monthly check, there will be surprisingly little that needs attention.

PROBLEM FILES

All lawyers have problem files – this may be because of a mental block, lack of time, lack of knowledge about what to do next, procrastination, dislike of that particular job or client – whatever the reason. The firm must make it a policy that it is not a disgrace to have problem files **but it is a cardinal sin to hide them!**

Recognise that there will be problem files and be open for your people to come up front and tell you that there is a problem. Bring it out into the open – in fact, make it easy for them to bring it out into the open. A problem for one lawyer is often a challenge for another.

With a new pair of eyes, the new lawyer can ring the other side and say, "Look, John Smith, who has been handling this matter, is on holiday/ill/away today. I've taken over the file. May I come and see you to agree a settlement on this matter – how about 3pm this afternoon or would sometime on Thursday suit you better?" Create some movement on it and turn those problem files into challenges – and then solutions.

GET MOVING!

No longer can lawyers sit back and watch as others move. Lawyers must be proactive. They must welcome change. They must be adaptable. Encourage the idea that new approaches are good. The old ways are not to be regarded as inviolable. Do not allow others to steal a march on you. If you have an idea to improve client relations, get moving on it straight away. Do not let the idea become bogged down in the committee system. You don't know what will work until you try it. So **try it** – but quickly.

LINK UP

For your larger clients, you need to be thinking in terms of linking with them so that they can contact you via e-mail. If you are not already deeply into e-mail, find out more about it and join in. It is the medium of today for swift and accurate communication. Tell your big clients that you welcome them contacting you this way. Be ready to embrace whatever technology next throws up – the advances are swift and impressive.

FAST SERVICE

Find ways to speed up the service you have. Clients **want** speed these days. They do not often **need** it but they certainly want it – so you must provide it.

- Be the fastest will provider in town and boast about it to all and sundry. Clients do not like thinking about their wills anyway so, the less time it takes you to prepare one for them, the better they will like it.

• Send those draft leases out the same day.

If you have doubt about the speed that clients seek, have a think about the photo developers that are around. Years ago, you dropped your roll of film into Boots the Chemist and collected it a week or so later. Now the developers have found that the public want their films developed a lot faster. In one survey, 64% of the customers said that they wanted one-hour developing. So we have in-house developers at almost every quick-snap shop you can go to. For the majority of people, there is no reason whatsoever why the film should be developed in one hour instead of seven days. It is often the holiday snaps that you took and you really do not **need** to see within hours of coming off the plane. However, you do **want** them, so the facilities are there for you to have them. It costs a bit more to get that fast developing service, but people are prepared to **pay** for it.

Ensure that your services are streamlined so that you can provide the fast service – and increase your fees to take that into account. That speed, together with the added value of information, will super-please your clients.

WHAT DO YOU THINK THE CLIENT WANTS?

We all have our own built-in idea of what the client wants and we could be drastically wrong.

Ernst & Young, the accountants, found that the top priority of their clients was that the accountant should be 'nice, available and know my name'. There was nothing to do with their professional expertise or figure-crunching ability!

Fidelity Investments thought that 'return on investment' would be most important for their financial clients. It wasn't!

'Availability' and 'being nice' were on top of their clients' list.

A survey in American found that the doctors who had no bedside manner were more likely to get more negligence claims!

So it is the **process** of delivering the service that is perceived to be more important than the service itself.

To find out what your clients want, ask them – it does not have to be a formal survey of clients carried out by MORI. Ask a few clients in for an hour's chat, give them some refreshments and say to them, "What do you like about what we do and what don't you like about what we do?"

You should find that most clients are delighted to be asked and will help and suggest ideas for you. That at least is a start and a good one. It gives you information about your service quickly.

You can also extract more regular feedback from your clients by regularising this process. Try one or more of the following:

- **Survey the clients**

  Put down on paper some questions that you would like to know your clients views on. Send out the survey to the clients. Tell them that you are asking for their help. Most clients will be delighted to assist.

- **Focus Groups**

  Have a selected group of clients come in to the office on a regular basis and chew over particular topics.

- **Outside help**

  Have an outside firm conduct a survey of your top clients. They may say more to a third party than they would to you.

- **Checklist**

  At the end of each transaction for your client, ask them to complete a checklist of specific questions. Avoid making it too long. Make sure they have the option of putting their name on the checklist or not, and that you pay for the list to be returned.

- **Monthly File Check**
  For each one of your people, have a system of doing a quality check. You chose one of their files and telephone the client to see how well he is being treated. Give a reward to the lawyer whose client gives the best client care story.

Clients will usually participate in such enquiries, particularly if there is some sort of payoff for them such as an attractive desk calendar or 5% off their next bill! You will need to choose the clients quite carefully for such surveys - some will not be forthcoming and some may be strongly opposed to such activities. Equally, you should not choose only those clients who you think are likely to give positive, glowing responses – that could skew the results and give you a false reading of your apparent total success, leading to complacency and smugness.

PINCH SOMEBODY ELSE'S IDEA

I do recognise that this is an extreme idea for lawyers! However, it is one that you must grasp. Remember the concept, in order to achieve unusual results, sometimes you have to use unusual methods! Well, here is one for you.

As you wander round town or other people's offices, keep your eyes open. If you see an idea that might be useful for your practice, then grab it. Adopt and adapt. Make an immediate note of it so that you don't forget it, then get together with some of your colleagues and brainstorm the idea to see how you can adapt it to suit **your** firm. It can be anything, from the seating in the clients' waiting area to the colour of the desks, the use of pictures to a cleverly designed data-capture form. There is a **big** mental block for lawyers who try to do this and the traditionalists will bleat:

- It's **not the done thing** to pinch somebody else's idea!
- Unless it's invented here then we don't want it!
- What will the competition think if we do it?

- It's a second-hand idea!
- We only do stuff that's original!

Forget all that mind stuff! It is hard to think of a **really** new idea but easier to adopt and adapt an existing idea. You do not need to invent the wheel everyday. (If it is of any help to you, this is being done all the time by others – and it works!) So if you see a different way of organising the office, the file management, office furniture, staff relations, billing, telephone procedure, whatever it is, have a think about it, brainstorm it and adapt it to your firm.

If you do find an idea in another company's premises or organisation, that really appeals to you, change it slightly to fit your own   organisation, but write to acknowledge the source of the idea. Perhaps your enthusiasm for the idea and the fact that you have taken the trouble to write and say thank-you for the inspiration will make the other people think highly of you and consider you as a supplier of services. Obviously, you cannot crib ideas that are copyright (you do not have to be told that!) but slight re-vamping of a design, layout, colour-scheme, furnishing plan or whatever would not cause too much difficulty.

WHERE'S THE NEXT BRIGHT IDEA COMING FROM?

We have looked at the concept of adopting and adapting the ideas of others. But where do you go for these ideas? Answer – absolutely anywhere you want and preferably anywhere you don't want to go!

You will get some interesting ideas from the way that other lawyers run their practices. But the most important ones are out there waiting for you. Get out of your own profession and look at what others are doing. The hotel and catering industries have been trying to please their guests for a long, long time. They have learnt a thing or two. Have a look at what they do and see if there is anything there that you can adopt and adapt.

Be ready to find your inspiration from anywhere – any other industry or profession:

- Art Galleries
- Large city shops
- The Clothes Show Exhibition
- Cinemas
- Airports
- Cruises
- The Army, Navy, Air Force
- Foreign Legal offices
- Harrods
- Toilet Walls
- Caravan parks
- Companies
- Banks
- Industrial companies
- Manufacturing companies
- Product packaging
- Magazines

- Book Shops
- Country small shops
- Theatres
- Libraries
- Discos
- The Legal Aid Office
- The Land Registry
- Abroad!
- Chinese restaurants
- Night shelters
- Shops
- Accountants
- Building Societies
- Universities
- Hotels
- Advertisements
- Television

That is quite a list - a vast variety of places that you can visit to gain inspiration and that germ of an idea or a whole concept for better client service.

Ring another firm in a totally different area, one that you will never be in direct competition with and start a dialogue, preferably with someone at your own level in the firm. Swap ideas about marketing or running the firm. Remember though that, plus or minus 10%, most legal firms are already doing what you are doing. That is why you need to take your blinkers off and look at other professions and industries to see what they are doing and see if you can apply their marketing and ideas to your firm.

THINKING DIFFERENTLY!!

Thinking in different ways is something that comes hard to lawyers. That is why we have to use the help of outside experts. Here is an example of different thinking – have a serious look at this:

Question: Which of the following letters is the most out of place and why?

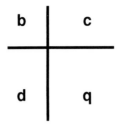

- Well, how did you get on? Did you think that 'c' doesn't fit because it has no straight line in the character itself?

- Did you think that it was 'q' because it is out of the sequence for the alphabet which included 'b', 'c' and 'd'?

- Maybe you thought it must be 'c' because the other three are just variations of the same character.

Have you considered the possibility that the answer could be 't'?!

Most of us haven't even spotted the 't'. In our daily lives we go about solving problems using the blinkered thoughts we already have. We work through the b's, c's and d's. We are looking for the conventional and not for something entirely different.

Try to be more creative. Have a good look at the other professions and industries and see how they work See what methods they have of attracting new clients and running their business. Adapt them to your firm and adopt them.

NOW!

INDEX